Lesley Vance & Ricky Swallow
at The Huntington

**Lesley Vance & Ricky Swallow
at The Huntington**

The Huntington Library, Art Collections, and
Botanical Gardens, San Marino, California

Major support for this project is provided by Laura and Carlton Seaver. Additional support is provided by the Philip and Muriel Berman Foundation; Margery and Maurice Katz; David Kordansky Gallery, Los Angeles; Stuart Shave/Modern Art, London; and Marc Foxx Gallery, Los Angeles.

Library of Congress Cataloging-in-Publication Data
Hess, Catherine, 1957–
    Lesley Vance and Ricky Swallow at the Huntington /
Catherine Hess, Christopher Bedford, and Suzanne Hudson.
      pages cm
    This book was published in conjunction with the exhibition
"Lesley Vance & Ricky Swallow at The Huntington," at The
Huntington Library, Art Collections, and Botanical Gardens
from November 10, 2012 through March 11, 2013.
    Includes bibliographical references.
    ISBN 978-0-87328-254-3 (alk. paper)
    1. Vance, Lesley, 1977– Exhibitions. 2. Swallow, Ricky, 1974–
Exhibitions. I. Bedford, Christopher. II. Hudson, Suzanne.
III. Vance, Lesley, 1977– Works. Selections. 2012. IV. Swallow,
Ricky, 1974– Works. Selections. 2012. V. Henry E. Huntington
Library and Art Gallery. VI. Title.
ND237.V145A4 2012
709.2'2—dc23   2012012713

Front cover: Photography by Fredrik Nilsen
Back cover: East side of the main staircase of the Huntington
residence. Reproduced by permission of the Huntington library,
San Marino, CA

Produced by Marquand Books, Inc., Seattle
  www.marquand.com

Edited by Martin Fox
Image management by iocolor, Seattle
Printed and bound in China by Artron Color Printing, Ltd.

Contents

Foreword

The installation of work by Lesley Vance and Ricky Swallow in the Huntington Art Gallery constitutes an important new venture for our institution. Although work by living artists has been displayed in other locations at The Huntington, and mainly in the gardens, this will be the first time it will appear in the mansion. When the Huntington Gallery —formerly Henry E. and Arabella Huntington's home—reopened to the public in 2008 after a three-year renovation, our visitors learned that rather than static presentations, these extraordinary private spaces on public display were vibrant and full of new discoveries. Even those who had long been associated with the institution said repeatedly that they were seeing artworks they'd never noticed before. Innovative juxtapositions and thematic groupings created new meanings and gave our visitors new reasons to return again and again.

It's in that spirit that we have embarked on this new experiment— installing a temporary exhibition of carefully selected contemporary work in a carefully developed space to further spur the spirit of delight and discovery. Our Chief Curator of European Art, Catherine Hess, deserves much credit for this, as it is a risky proposition indeed: The Huntington treads quite infrequently into the world of contemporary art and is not always perfectly comfortable doing so, especially given the strong contemporary art museums and galleries well established in Los Angeles. Nevertheless, we know there are, from time to time, opportunities here for connections to be made to the work of living artists. Recent exhibitions, in fact, have included displays of work by Allan Sekula, Louise Lawler, and John Frame. Contemporary art provides the opportunity for us to see our permanent collections in a new context, and with fresh eyes. And in this particular case, we feel certain that the rich associations with art of the past and the exploration of form, medium, and content make the paintings by Lesley Vance and sculpture by Ricky Swallow intriguing complements to the mansion's permanent display. We hope that the installation will stimulate curiosity and joy in the appreciation of these remarkable works in this remarkable place.

STEVEN KOBLIK, PRESIDENT
The Huntington Library, Art Collections, and Botanical Gardens

A Creative Act

Catherine Hess

The assembling of an art collection is a creative act. Great art collectors require vision and passion, qualities that count to a greater degree than any of the more prosaic interests that might come into play, such as investment potential or cultural validation. Arabella and Henry E. Huntington were great art collectors. Their history is ably told elsewhere.[1] Nevertheless, it is useful to recapitulate it briefly here.

Henry Edwards Huntington moved to San Francisco at the age of forty-two to help his uncle, railroad magnate Collis P. Huntington, manage the Southern Pacific Railroad. On a trip to Southern California, he visited a ranch in the San Gabriel Valley, northeast of Los Angeles, and fell in love with the property (fig. 1). Henry's attraction to the climate and the natural beauty of the area, coupled with his interest in the commercial and cultural potential of the region, led him to move to Los Angeles in 1902—two years after Collis's death—and buy the beloved ranch when the opportunity presented itself the following year.

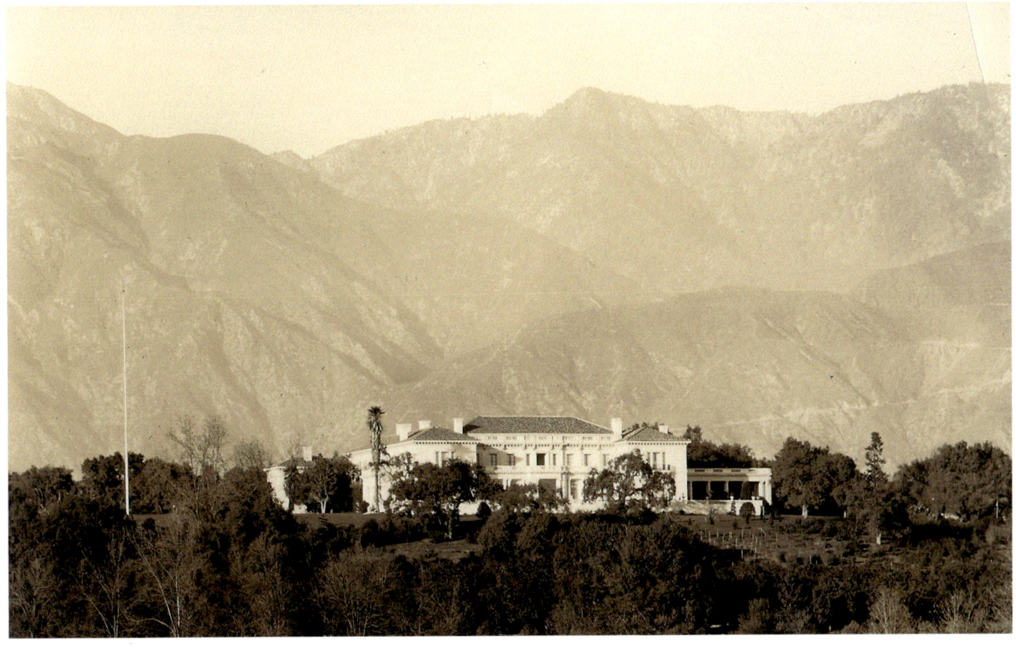

Fig. 1
The Huntington residence from the south, set against the San Gabriel Mountains, circa 1911–12. Reproduced by permission of the Huntington Library, San Marino, CA

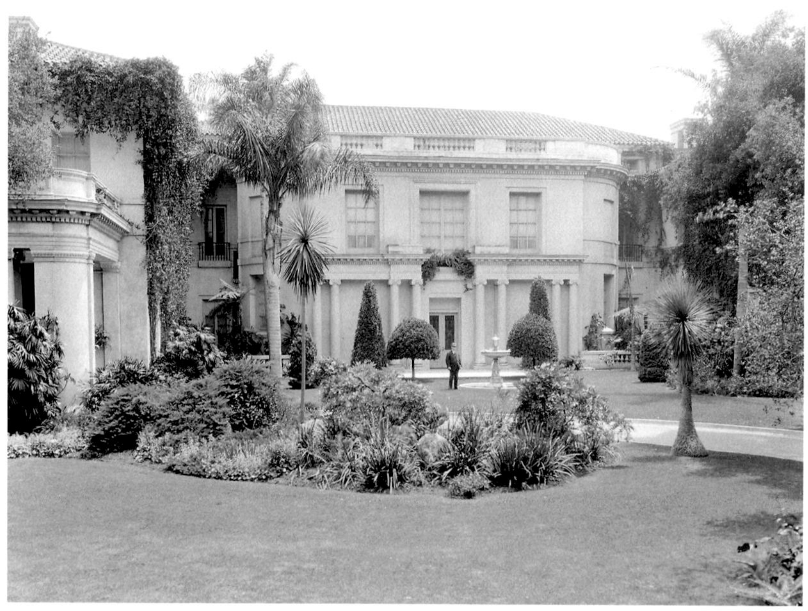

Fig. 2 Henry E. Huntington standing in front of the north façade of the Huntington residence, circa 1915. Reproduced by permission of the Huntington Library, San Marino, CA

In 1910, at the age of sixty, Huntington began to devote most of his time to the collecting of rare books, a lifelong passion. While his book collection was growing, Henry Huntington was also developing an interest in art, influenced in large part by Arabella Huntington, Collis's widow, with whom he had become personally involved following Collis's death. His art collecting accelerated just at this time. She was one of the wealthiest women in America and one of the most important collectors of her generation. Henry and Arabella eventually married in 1913 when they were both in their early sixties.

Henry hired the Pasadena architecture firm of Myron Hunt and Elmer Grey to design the San Marino residence, which was to serve as a part-time home. Construction began in 1908 and the Huntingtons finally occupied their Beaux-Arts style residence in 1914 (fig. 2). Five years later, with the intention of eventually opening the collection to the public, Henry and Arabella transferred the property and collections to a nonprofit trust. Following Arabella's death in 1924 and Henry's in 1927, the institution opened to the public in 1928 (figs. 3, 4).

Their collecting activity was in accord with the standards of Gilded Age taste—eighteenth-century British and French painting and decorative arts as well as a smattering of Italian works of art—as advocated by their primary art dealer, Joseph Duveen. While these standards were popular as a means of linking newly rich Americans with an august past, more mundane circumstances influenced what they collected. These circumstances

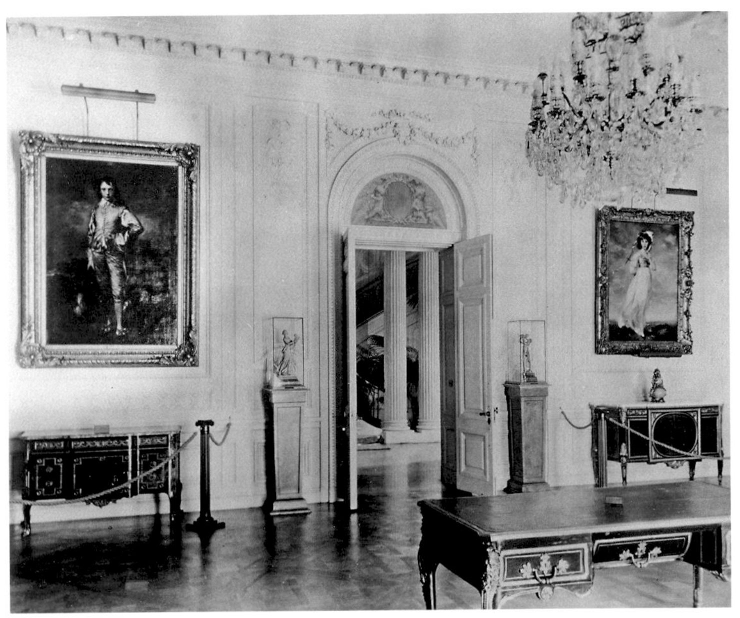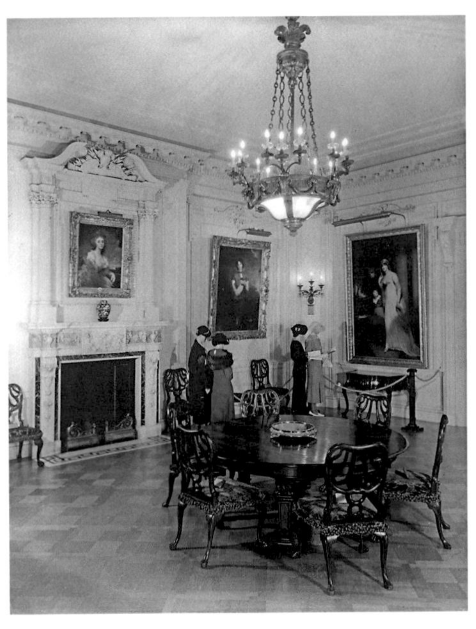

Fig. 3 Large drawing room in the Huntington residence. The image was published in the *Los Angeles Times,* January 2, 1930. Reproduced by permission of the Huntington Library, San Marino, CA

Fig. 4 Dining Room in the Huntington residence soon after opening to the public in 1928. Reproduced by permission of the Huntington Library, San Marino, CA

included increased access to European art coming on to the market; a new and vibrant art market that capitalized on the unprecedented wealth they and their fellow industrialists accumulated during the second half of the nineteenth century; and a new affordability of imported works of art thanks to the repeal of certain tariffs. Within this new arena, Duveen proved to be ever perceptive and opportunistic. He "noticed that Europe had plenty of art and America had plenty of money and his astonishing career was the product of that simple observation."[2]

Other than what was available, why such an emphasis on British and French art? Henry's penchant for British art probably grew out of an interest in British material for his library. Might Arabella's Francophilia be traceable to the fact that her grandmother was French, whose surname—Duval—she carried as her middle name? Certainly, she was following in the path of notable British collectors of the early nineteenth century whose interest in French eighteenth-century art sprung from the desire to be linked with the French *ancien régime.* The taste for this material continued into the late nineteenth century as displayed in such aristocratic British residences as the Wallace Collection and Waddesdon Manor, both of which served as important models for Henry and Arabella.

Within this collecting scheme, they appear to have been only marginally concerned with either art of their time or American art, with a few notable exceptions. They acquired a bronze sculpture of a *Bacchante and Infant Faun* directly from its American artist, Frederick MacMonnies, who also advised on the placement of the sculpture among cycads just northeast of the mansion, where it stands today. In addition, a pair of carved stone dogs by Arabella's daughter-in-law and Henry's niece by marriage, Anna Hyatt Huntington, entered the collection in 1923.

American art interested them to the degree that it related to their other collecting areas. His adopted home in the American West inspired Henry to acquire contemporary photographs by Carl Moon and Frederick Monsen, while presidential portraits—in photographs, paintings, and sculpture—aligned with Henry's library holdings. Paintings by Anglo-American John Singleton Copley and Benjamin West, and furniture by Franco-American Charles Honoré Lannuier fit in well with their other works of art.[3]

What sense, then, does an installation of contemporary American art have in the setting of the Huntington mansion?

All art was at one time contemporary. For Henry and Arabella, the most significant contemporary work of art on their San Marino property was the house itself, as it continues to be in the narrative of the place. When it was built, the mansion constituted a remarkable addition to the landscape of southern California. Not only was it one of the first important examples of Beaux-Arts architecture in the region but also, at 35,000 square feet, it remained the region's largest residence for many decades.

Little is known about the disposition of art and furnishings in the mansion. And although room-by-room inventories were compiled after Henry's death in 1927, no photograph remains of the interior spaces from the time the couple inhabited them. A few photos document gorgeous exterior views from 1915 to 1920, but only one records an interior view, of the dining room, set for a luncheon with the Crown Prince of Sweden in July 1926, two years after Arabella's death and one before Henry's (fig. 5). The paintings on the walls in that photograph tell us that before the Portrait Gallery was constructed in the early 1930s, the Grand Manner portraits crowded the smaller-scale domestic settings. The dining room retains its early twentieth-century chandelier—matching the corner wall lights that remain in the room—that was replaced with an eighteenth-century crystal one in 1959. The space appears ornate and varied, formal yet inviting.

Why Arabella and Henry chose not to document the carefully constructed and installed interiors may be explained by their interest in privacy and their conception of the place as a supremely private home, not intended for the parties one might associate with other Gilded Age mansions. Nevertheless, their synthesized amalgam of art, decoration, and architecture must have been purposeful and personalized, though it was certainly less quixotic than those of Isabella Stewart Gardner in her Fenway Park home, Albert Barnes in his Merion, Pennsylvania, complex, or Louise and Walter Arensberg in their Hollywood residence.[4]

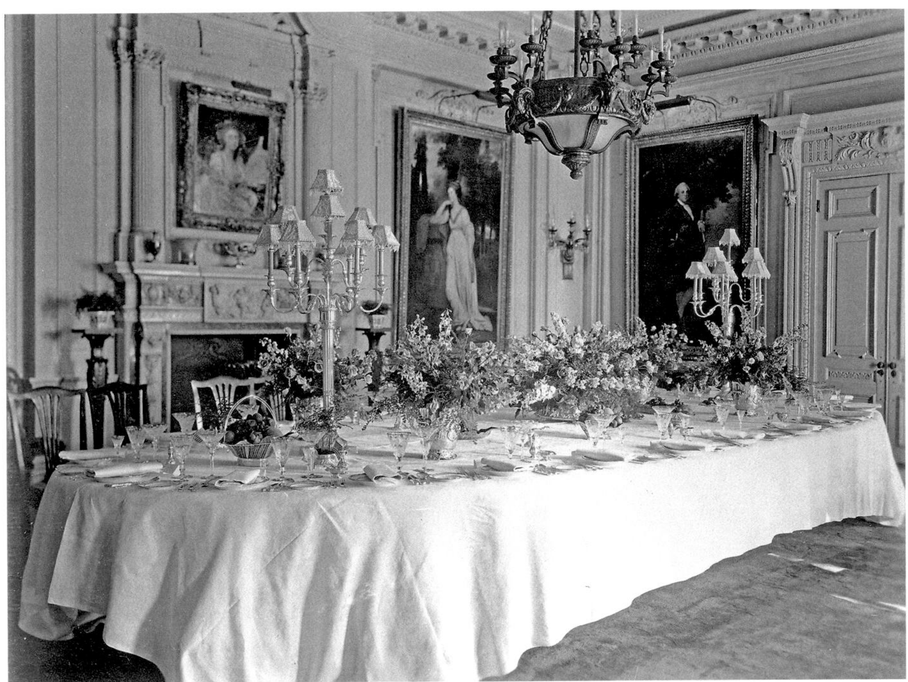

Fig. 5 Dining Room in the Huntington residence set for a luncheon, July 1926.
Reproduced by permission of the Huntington Library, San Marino, CA

Henry and Arabella reinstalled their collection as it grew and surely they organized the displays in intentional groupings to create relationships among the works and within the design of the house. Their collection was a growing and shifting ensemble, creatively conceived and assembled, varying with changes in circumstance and desire, and set against the architectural backdrop of their house. Although little is known about what those displays looked liked, much less signified, curatorial interventions and acquisitions since the house opened to the public in 1928 continue the creative process of display. Additions are made to engage with the Huntingtons' collections in ways that enhance and enlarge their original vision. Two of the most significant are surely Anthony van Dyck's *Anne (Killigrew) Kirke* of about 1637, acquired in 1983, and Joseph Wright of Derby's *Vesuvius from Portici* of about 1774–76, acquired in 1997. These works effectively communicate with other works of art around them so that the public is encouraged, by their very presence and through effective textual information, to create thoughtful links and meanings, be they intellectual, visual, or personal.

Such is the intent of the display of artwork by Lesley Vance and Ricky Swallow. Like Arabella and Henry, they are married to one another, and, like Arabella and Henry, they have distinct creative visions. Nevertheless, sharing studio space provides Vance and Swallow the opportunity to assess and discuss their work with one another. To what degree conjugality and propinquity affect the results is an interesting question.

Since theirs is a temporary installation, the presentation can be more eccentric, provocative, and challenging than any longer-term addition to the Huntington's permanent collection. This situation is a special and valuable one. It allows for a vital and lively examination of the surrounding painting, sculpture, decorative arts, and architecture. Both Vance's and Swallow's work links with artwork of the past: Old Master paintings, patinated bronzes, still lifes, glazed ceramics, objects of virtue. Their presence among the Huntington's collections will strike a familiar note while, perhaps, provoking new associations and evaluations.

1   Shelley M. Bennett, "The Formation of Henry E. Huntington's Collection of British Paintings," in *British Paintings at The Huntington,* ed. Robyn Asleson and Shelley M. Bennett (New Haven, CT: Yale University Press, 2001), 1–15; Shelley M. Bennett, "Henry and Arabella Huntington: The Staging of Eighteenth-Century French Art by Twentieth-Century Americans," in *French Art of the Eighteenth Century at The Huntington,* ed. Shelley M. Bennett and Carolyn Sargentson (New Haven, CT: Yale University Press, 2007), 1–27.

2   S. N. Behrman, *Duveen* (London: Hamish Hamilton, 1952), 1.

3   My thanks to Jenny Watts, Curator of Photographs, the Huntington Library; and Jessica Todd Smith, Chief Curator of American Art, the Huntington Art Collections, for the information they provided on these points.

4   See, for example, Nicolai Ouroussoff, "Eccentricity Gives Way to Uniformity in Museums," *New York Times,* March 26, 2011; available online: *http://www.nytimes.com/2011/03/27/weekinreview/27ouroussof.html;* and Naomi Sawelson-Gorse, "'For the Want of a Nail': The Disposition of the Louise and Walter Arensberg Collection" (master's thesis, University of California, Riverside, 1987).

The Surface of Circumstance

Suzanne Hudson

A man holding a black umbrella stands inconspicuously amid a throng of spectators, despite the incongruity of his attribute. The citizen, incidentally recorded by the home-movie camera of Abraham Zapruder, might have supplied an inconsequential detail in a prosaic community pageant were it not for the exigencies that brought the film to public attention in the first place. (It famously captures John F. Kennedy's motorcade passing through Dealey Plaza in Dallas on November 22, 1963, offering a largely unobstructed and especially gruesome vantage of the president's assassination.) Like many of his generation, John Updike was compelled by the so-called umbrella man's presence in the Zapruder images, as well as the myriad conspiracy theories in which he subsequently assumed a prominent role. This sentinel lingered, in the writer's words, like a "fetish"—an empirical fact and estimation of what might remain beyond it. In a dazzling passage, Updike poses: "We wonder whether a genuine mystery is being concealed here or whether any similar scrutiny of a minute section of time and space would yield similar strangenesses—gaps, inconsistencies, warps, and bubbles in the surface of circumstance."[1]

I came across this quote recently and distractedly; but once I read it, I couldn't let it go. It so happened that I was thinking about Lesley Vance's practice and the apposition of these words to her small canvases came to seem inevitable. More than any critical writing on the historical still life or its contemporary manifestations, Updike's musings about this celluloid frame approach the inherent peculiarity of really *looking* that Vance's paintings perform as method and manage as pictorial effect. Surfaces of circumstance felicitously illustrate the conditional coming together of objects in the representational field. And Updike's description—tinged as it is with a kind of morbidity—finds comparable expression in the heightened vulnerability of the genre's mainstays: ripe fruit and foodstuff anticipatorily shown before consumption or flora in full bloom awaiting detumescence. It is striking the extent to which these issues obtain even in Vance's recent abstract paintings, begun in 2009, which eschew the direct translation of thing into pigment that characterized her prior efforts in more conventional still life.

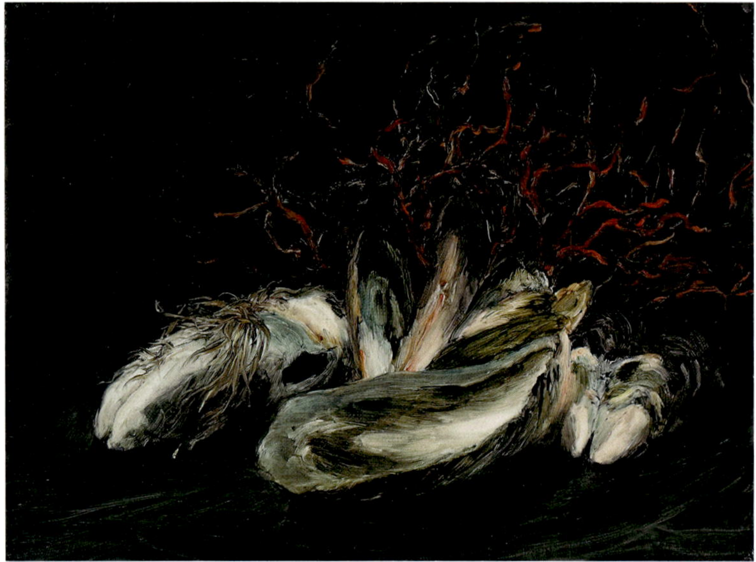

Fig. 6 Lesley Vance
Mussels, Coral Frond, 2007
Oil on linen, 8 × 11 inches
Private Collection

In formative pieces like *Mussels, Coral Frond* (fig. 6) and *Four Poppies* (fig. 7), both painted in 2007, Vance offered glimpses of a world greeted at arm's length, patiently transcribed in all of its sensuousness (the glistening opalescence of the clams; the intense vermillion of the flowers). But to say "direct translation," as I just did, is not quite right, because these and other examples betray Vance's explicit self-consciousness in facture-laden passages where her brush lingered and went sketchy, thereby obfuscating some detail that it might have clarified. (One could propose that Vance exposes a dynamic central to modernism as critic Clement Greenberg understood it, namely the using of art to call attention to, rather than conceal, the nature of art: "The limitations that constitute the medium of painting—the flat surface, the shape of the support, the properties of the pigment—were treated by the Old Masters as negative factors that could be acknowledged only implicitly or indirectly. Under Modernism these same limitations came to be regarded as positive factors, and were acknowledged openly.")[2] Vance makes clear the conceits framing the act of still-life painting. The careful arrangements—or items spied in isolation—that emerge out of velveteen black backgrounds recall such seventeenth-century Spanish painters as Juan Sanchez Cotán and Francisco de Zurburán. Indeed, these allusions are so direct that the act of appropriation itself becomes a kind of subject.

Vance since has maintained a commitment to staging the contingency of relationships, though on different terms: Whereas the still-life figures these interactions as representational order (a quince just caressed by an apple adjacent to it), her abstractions recast them as process. Vance begins by selecting objects from her curio-cabinet-like storehouse. She then assembles them to be photographed in a resolutely low-tech cardboard box outfitted for diverse lighting scenarios. The photo becomes the

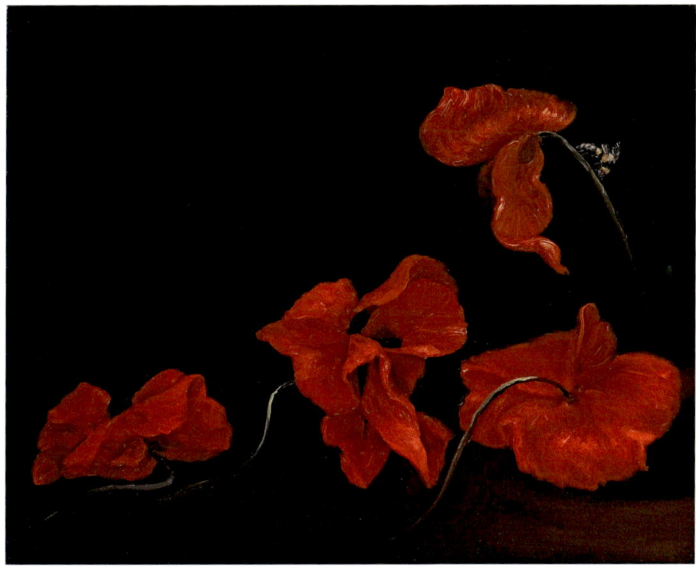

Fig. 7 Lesley Vance
Four Poppies, 2007
Oil on linen, 11 × 14 inches
Collection of Joshua Adler,
New York

basis for the painting, which wrests from such tangible articles—shells, horns, a piece of coral, a ceramic jar—a series of formal passages akin to cubist dissections. Although decision-making is clearly key to achieving coruscating tints and fugitive effects of light and shadow in such shallow space—and at such a small scale—the paintings do not offer themselves up in such a way as to demonstrate either the sequence or intentionality of these choices. Instead, the fact that Vance's brush moved here not there, revealing this peach not that umber, is upheld as the mystery of the straightforward course so clearly announced at the outset: gather, shoot, labor in a single sitting, over the span of hours, with paint deposited onto wet paint.

Thus does narrative become a matter of technique—how the work came to be as a material fact, not to what it refers. (Nonetheless, as in the instance of the umbrella man, there is a remainder beyond this obdurate presence that manages, like uncanny surrealist juxtapositions before it, to unsettle.) In, say, *Untitled,* of 2012 (fig. 8), we cannot excavate what engendered it (that is, we cannot determine its sources, which are made exogenous to the work; we cannot find the still life, even as we know it started things in motion, even as we appreciate that it generated the non-objective structure that now serves in its place). In rare instances, we gain hold of intimations of these forbearers through the contour of a shape or the spectrum of a palette—experiences of what Willem de Kooning called glimpses of content, "an encounter like a flash."[3] More commonly, we are left with the fact of the paint pushed into its current arrangement, and the question of how, especially as the paint typically sits, all surface, as a single layer—again, the result of Vance working it over such a short course of time. Swatches of linen weave visible through palette knife-scraped paint provide one rejoinder, but Vance avoids global transparency. Even

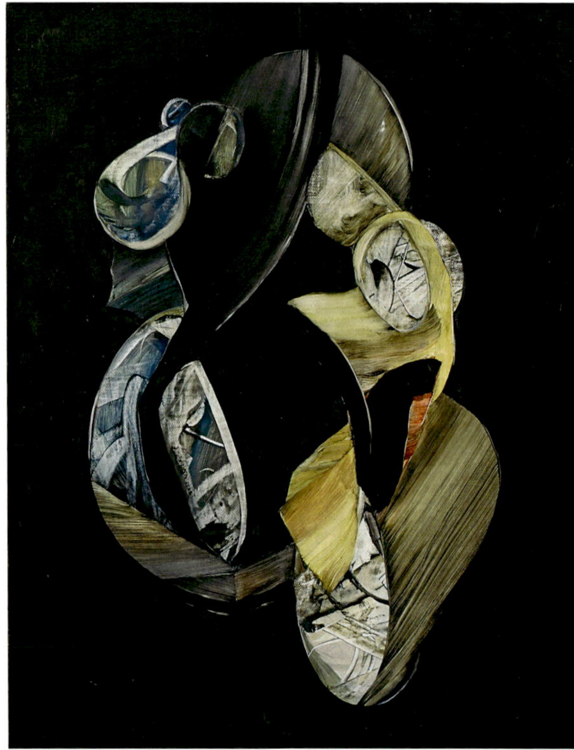

Fig. 8 Lesley Vance
Untitled, 2012
Oil on linen, 18 × 14 inches

her related charcoal, watercolor, and gouache drawings on vellum, which record her play with the primary elements at varying stages, bear little resemblance to the paintings.

Perhaps this lingering sense of inscrutability owes to Vance's courting of the aleatory for herself, as maker and her own first viewer. Despite the circumscription of the act within the parameters of scenario and temporal duration, there is neither a telos to some anticipated end (as there is in a composition determined a priori) nor a knowable outcome. There is only, at best, a provisional stasis that results from Vance's calling it quits for the day—and leaving the painting in that design ever after. In this, Vance's abstractions are built on the logic of suspension. Each painting depicts— and comes to rest on—a state of transformation poised between what brought it into being and where it might still go. Caught where it is, fixed at a determinate moment, each one is, too, an artifact emblematic of the fleeting precariousness long associated with still life.

This raises the question, which Vance solicits in the paintings and put forward to me in conversation: What would it mean for abstraction to "bring you in like a representational painting"?[4] It might mean, for one, assuming still life as the point of comparison (as is true for Vance), that we enter a pictorial space supposing its intimacy and finding, as a byproduct of the weirdness of the world observed at such a proximate range and with such intensity, the dilations, puckers, warps, and incongruities coin- cident with that peculiar realm of the sensate to which John Updike had recourse. It likewise raises a very interesting inverse problem—answered in one way by Clement Greenberg—namely how the intercession of abstraction transforms our perception of representational painting, Old Master or otherwise. The art historian Christopher Wood writes: "Abstraction implores us to look at the rest of painting as if it were abstract. In Meyer Schapiro's paradoxical formulation, realism itself re-created the world by a 'series of abstract calculations of perspective and gradations of color.' . . . Abstraction, it appears, was never anything more than a refinement or a mannered distortion of the components of painted art, totally consistent with the previous history of painting, and capable of very many of its effects."[5]

Vance's abstractions, built as they are on a still life mediated by a photograph only to be let loose from the burdens of semblance, claim abstraction and representation to exist on a continuum. The latter yields the disorientation of specific entity into color and shape, even as the former makes that plastic space stunningly real. To be sure, Vance tempers an impulse toward autonomous painting (long associated with abstraction's eschewal of the mimetic) with an equal imperative to locate it within the tradition of three-dimensional rendering, so reliant on skills of manipulating light and color, shading and shadow, and so on, to create pictorial illusions. However, Vance stops short of denying objecthood; instead, she everywhere highlights the physicality of the linen and the reality of its surface alike. This emphasis is, finally, what gives the notion of the surface of circumstance such interpretive weight: What is brought into being there is not incidental or dematerialized, but insistently present, bearing actual holes (and startling depths) alongside its conjured ones. For Vance, still life facilitates abstraction, which, in turn, divulges the abstraction subtending a representational articulation of appearance. We are left with paintings about painting as a site of material and conceptual convention; even more, these are paintings that, at their best, in their insistence on the consequence of bearing down on a "minute section of time and space," train us to really see.

1   John Updike, "Comment," *New Yorker,* December 9, 1967, 51. Quoted in Jon Michaud, "Updike, J. F. K. and the Umbrella Man," *New Yorker,* November 22, 2011, http://www .newyorker.com/online/blogs/backissues/2011/11/john-updike-jfk-assassination-the -umbrella-man.html.

2   Clement Greenberg, "Modernist Painting," in *Clement Greenberg: The Collected Essays and Criticism,* vol. 4, *Modernism with a Vengeance, 1957–1969,* ed. John O'Brian (1960; Chicago: The University of Chicago Press, 1993), 86.

3   Willem de Kooning, "Content Is a Glimpse," in *Willem de Kooning: The Collected Writings,* ed. George Scrivani (1963; Madras and New York: Hanuman Books, 1988), 83.

4   Lesley Vance in conversation with the author, December 19, 2011.

5   Christopher S. Wood, "Ryman's Poetics," *Art in America* 82, no. 1 (January 1994): 67–68. See also Meyer Schapiro, "Nature of Abstract Art," in *Modern Art: Nineteenth and Twentieth Centuries* (1937; New York: George Braziller, 1978), 196.

A Replacement of Its Former Self

Christopher Bedford

In 1950 and then again in 1951, David Smith received a John Simon Guggenheim Memorial Foundation Fellowship, an award that permitted the artist to set aside, at least temporarily, his teaching responsibilities and commit himself unfettered to the studio. Unsurprisingly, those years proved productive for Smith, yielding at least three enduring masterpieces: *Australia* (1951), *Hudson River Landscape* (1951), and *The Letter* (1950) (fig. 9). Variously interpreted as a series of deliberately unintelligible glyphs, a plea to an ex-lover, a transcription of the famous letter in James Joyce's *Finnegan's Wake,* and a note to his mother about Ohio, *The Letter* is above all and most vitally a translation of one thing into another. *The Letter* is made intelligible as such by an inscription and a salutation that bracket a body of text made up of what Smith called "object symbols."[1] Yet everything Smith achieves in the work turns the traditional function of the letter on its head: the weightlessness of paper is given the heft and rigidity of steel, its fundamental portability nullified, the object tethered to the earth by a base; the letter's opening salutation is reduced to an abstract squiggle in space; and the body of the text does not communicate via a shared language, but dumbfounds with a succession of hermetic symbols known only to the author. The only element that can be easily understood as content is the signature, and not because the words are easily read, but because Smith's autographic mark is eminently recognizable as an image (or brand), making language, in turn, irrelevant. Smith, then, takes a form—the letter—with a standard cultural application defined by language, and denies that conventional utility, making it function only as an image to be looked at.

That the Australian-born sculptor Ricky Swallow would feel a kinship with David Smith and with *The Letter* in particular should come as no surprise to anyone familiar with the former's work. Consider the following quotes, the first from Swallow and the second from Smith:

> Growing up around a more working-class environment, the closest things
> to sculpture I was exposed to were the crafts related to the fishing profes-
> sion my father was involved in—cray pots (lobster baskets) made from
> tea tree limbs, lead net weights poured into molds in our yard, or my

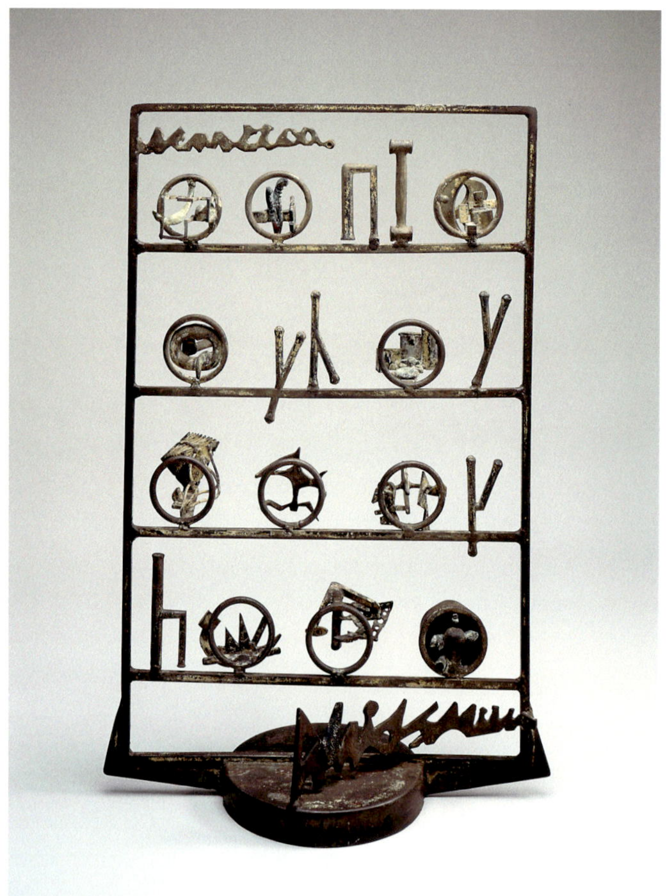

Fig. 9 David Smith
The Letter, 1950
Welded steel, 37⅝ × 22⅞ × 9¼ in.
Munson-Williams-Proctor Arts
Institute, Utica, NY

father's welded cube structures for storing ropes . . . there was always this anxious necessity to keep oneself occupied . . . So I went off to art school with a fairly limited understanding of what constitutes being an artist, yet this observed daily ritual of work—of stubborn traditions followed and rudimentary materials employed—was something I adopted myself and I still believe in those basic principles . . . "hands out of pockets!" as my father would say.[2]

The mystic modeling clay in only Ohio mud, the tools are at hand in garages and factories. Casting can be achieved in almost every town. Visions are from the imaginative mind, sculpture can come from the found discards in nature, from sticks and stones and parts and pieces, assembled or monolithic, solid form, open form, lines of form, or, like a painting, the illusion of form.[3]

Both artists point resolutely to a philosophy of making that is grounded practically and ideologically in the labor activities of the working class, and to the materials, objects, tools, and processes of that world as the literal genesis of their efforts to forge a new world of images, a world of and about the one we all occupy. Smith believed that work begets work, and Swallow shares that conviction. But while both artists champion the notion of a laboring class, and count themselves as workers, their respective stagings of that position are somewhat different. As a practicing artist, Smith's relationship to the working class ideal was intentionally indexical, hinging on a set of processes and materials that related directly to the physical work done by men in foundries and factories, men with whom he felt a deep affinity. That Swallow shares Smith's investment in the virtues and value of work is clear, but his materials and processes do not parallel the labor performed by working men in the same way. Instead, the link back to "common people and common things" is actuated on the level of imagery, or as Swallow notes, "ritual" acts and objects familiar and accessible to all.

Take, for instance, Swallow's interest in domestic subjects, particularly vessels. *Stacking Cup/Tapered (Bone),* 2011, is a modest object, measuring 4¼ × 5¼ × 4¼ inches—domestically scaled, one might say—cast in bronze and then patinated, in an edition of three with one artist's proof. Like many of his most recent vessels, the object is sketched from memory using a flexible system of cardboard and tape, its form continually embellished and improvised to eventually yield a splintered vision of its former self. Once cast and patinated—this one a soft, matte white—the surface of the object faithfully captures its deliberately rough means of construction; the imperfect joins in the cardboard and folds in the tape mark out a peculiar kind of facture that has become Swallow's signature. Quite clearly, then, neither mimesis nor trompe-l'oeil are of interest to the artist. His effort isn't to faithfully reproduce a likeness, but to denote the process of thinking and working from the quotidian to the quietly extraordinary; from the observed world, to something other. The central principle at work here is the same one that governs Smith's *The Letter,* namely translation: the process by which the artist makes of the familiar and useful, an object that is markedly neither.

While Smith relied on his processes and materials to tether his work to the working milieu that was his intended point of reference, Swallow's approach to the same idea is, as we've already seen, more oblique and less specific. He gravitates to objects defined by what he calls an air of "collective ownership," their utter familiarity as things in the world making them particularly effective as blank canvases for the imposition of new meaning.[4] Though working-class ethics, craft, and tools may be his point of reference, his objects signify more democratically than that, being everyday and common in the broadest sense. As a result, perhaps, Swallow's work exerts a magnetism that seems disproportionate to his choice of subject matter; one might even say that his sculptures should not be as interesting as they are! *Single Pot with Lid (Bone/Soot),* 2011, could be a teapot or a shrunken watering can—old, discarded, or hurriedly fixed up to extend its life just a little. But the pot and the lid, both cast in bronze with a delicate white patina, sit atop two bronze pedestals cast from sawn wooden blocks,

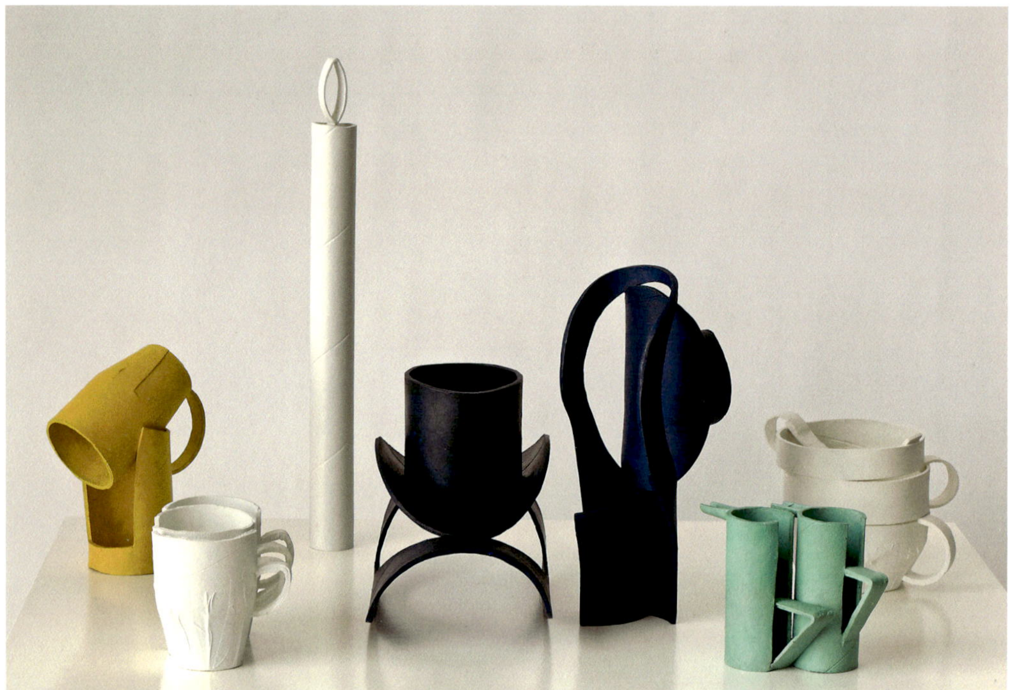

Fig. 10 Ricky Swallow, Installation view, the artist's studio, Los Angeles, 2011

signifying immediately their status as objects to be looked at. As a still life, *Single Pot with Lid (Bone/Soot)* conforms to the basic conventions of the genre in that it proposes the forthrightly mundane as an object for contemplation. But this sculpture, like much of Swallow's work, scrupulously avoids the laden symbolism associated with the highest achievements of the genre. His assemblies do not, for instance, follow in the footsteps of Netherlandish vanitas painting of the sixteenth and seventeenth century, or the Renaissance memento mori tradition, and nor, for that matter, does he appear interested in advancing the radical formal experiments enacted on the genre during the artistic ferment of the early twentieth century. If Swallow has a kinsman within the ranks of the still-life tradition, that person might be the Italian painter Giorgio Morandi, who, like Swallow, returned again and again to the same subjects, but even this comparison, while formally apposite, lacks any deeper logic.

Single Pot with Lid (Bone/Soot), and many other works like it, command one's total attention not because they are allegorical, represent a self-evidently important subject, advance a wildly radical formal agenda, are pointedly topical or political, or trade in the easy appeal of modern-day spectacle. Rather, they embody the possibility—modestly and simply— of pure invention: a message made all the more accessible, direct, and resonant because Swallow performs his transformations on the most commonplace objects, objects available and used by each of us daily.

When he reimagines the form of a lamp in *Table Lamp Study (Cadmium Yellow),* 2011—casting his cardboard invention in bronze, and finishing the composition in yellow—the resultant proposition is remarkable precisely because Swallow wrings the elusively new from the familiar with the opposite of extravagance. The same applies to the aforementioned *Single Pot with Lid (Bone/Soot).* Perched atop their diminutive black monoliths, the two components are quiet and unassuming in their scale and subject; yet in the curiousness of their construction and in their subtly orchestrated flirtation with familiarity and utility, they achieve the same autonomy as objects that Smith achieved so memorably with *The Letter.* If one of Smith's objectives was to parlay the life, ethics, and materials of the working man into the basis for a life in art, then Swallow's still-evolving practice might be understood as a comparable effort to demystify art-making—to strip it of its hermeticism and specialization—and argue through his own subjects and working processes that everyday contexts and the most incidental objects can be the basis for a compelling idea; in other words, to make aesthetic ideas seamless with the common world in a very concrete sense.

Ricky Swallow builds himself into the material world through this method of translation, complicating common objects through his labor, inscribing in them a new order of meaning that has everything to do with his eye, mind, and hand, and little to do with the object's former outward signification. What they were made *for* is now immaterial; what matters now is *how* they were made and that they demand a new kind of attention. The artist himself notes: "this economy of labor and materials toward something that's a translation of a traditional object, a replacement of its former self, is something I love."[5] As Swallow works to further populate *his* world of former selves, the force of his ideas and the reach of his vision into *our* world become more and more apparent.

<hr>

1   David Smith, quoted in *David Smith: A Centennial,* ed. Carmen Giménez (New York: The Solomon R. Guggenheim Foundation, 2006), 404.

2   Ricky Swallow, e-mail message to the author, March 12, 2012.

3   David Smith, "Tradition and Identity," transcript of a speech given on April 17, 1959, at Ohio University in Athens, Ohio, which Smith attended for a year in 1924–25, http://www.davidsmithestate.org/statements.html.

4   Ricky Swallow, "500 Words," *Artforum,* Jan. 30, 2011, http://artforum.com/words /id=27455.

5   Swallow, "500 Words."

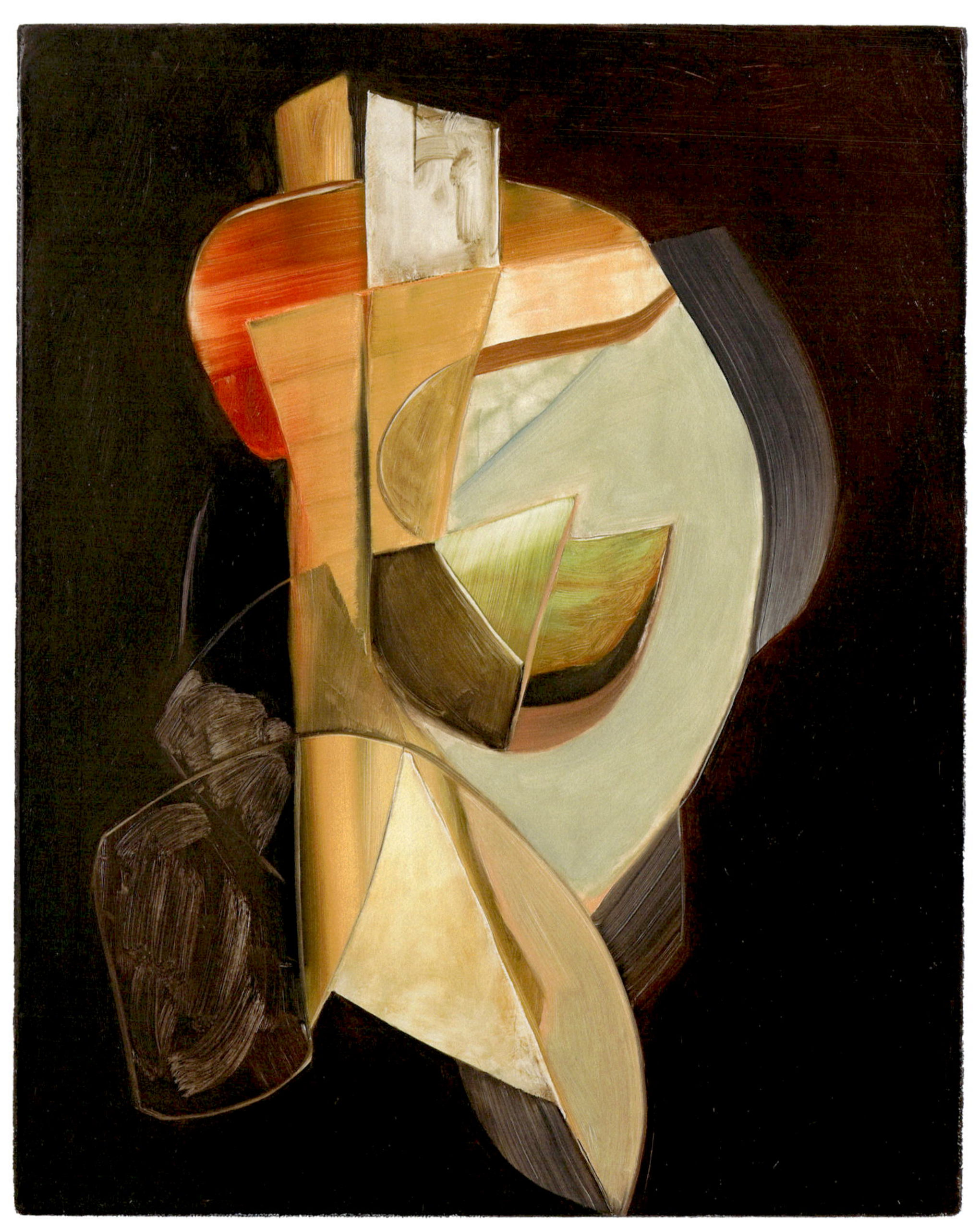

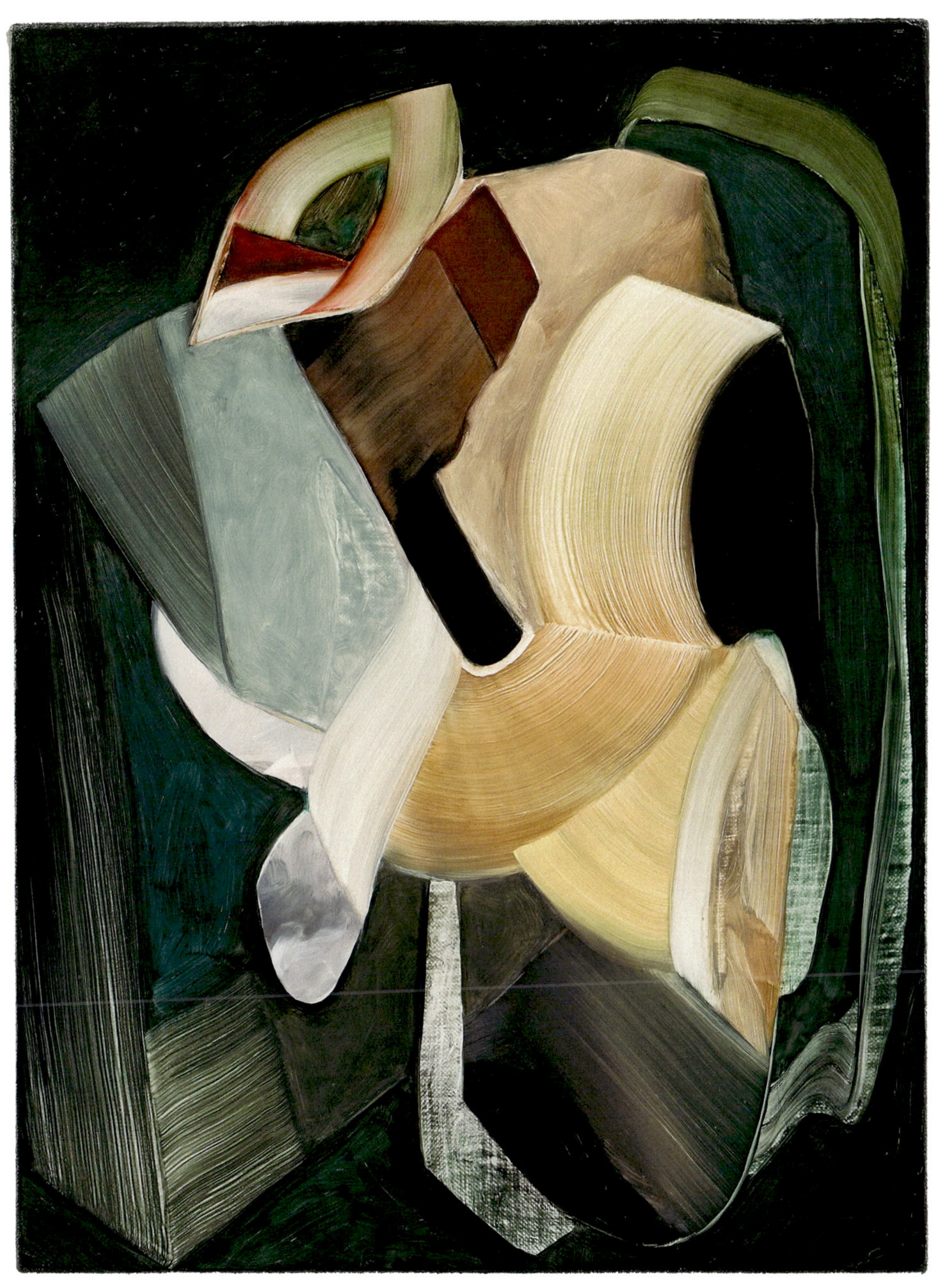

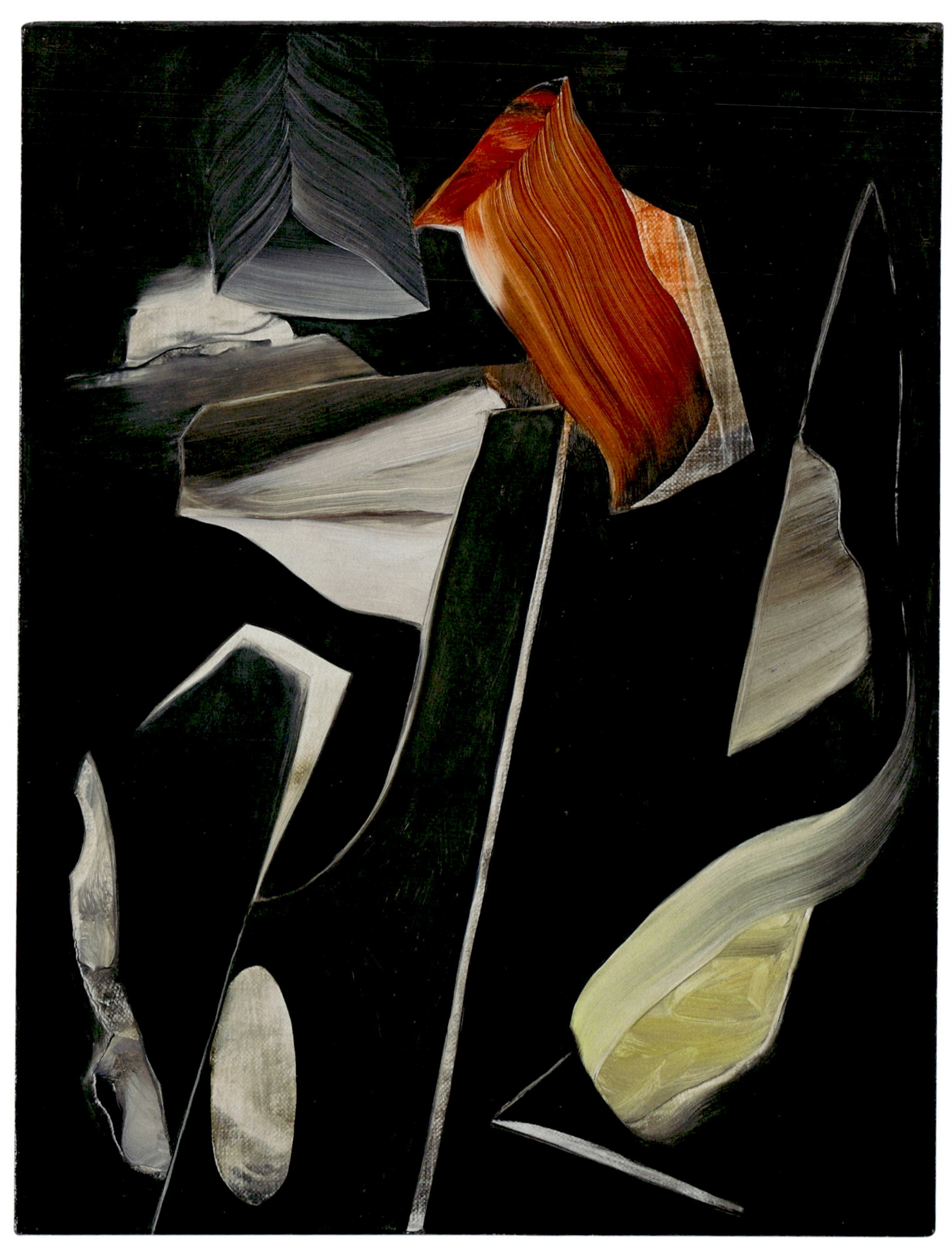

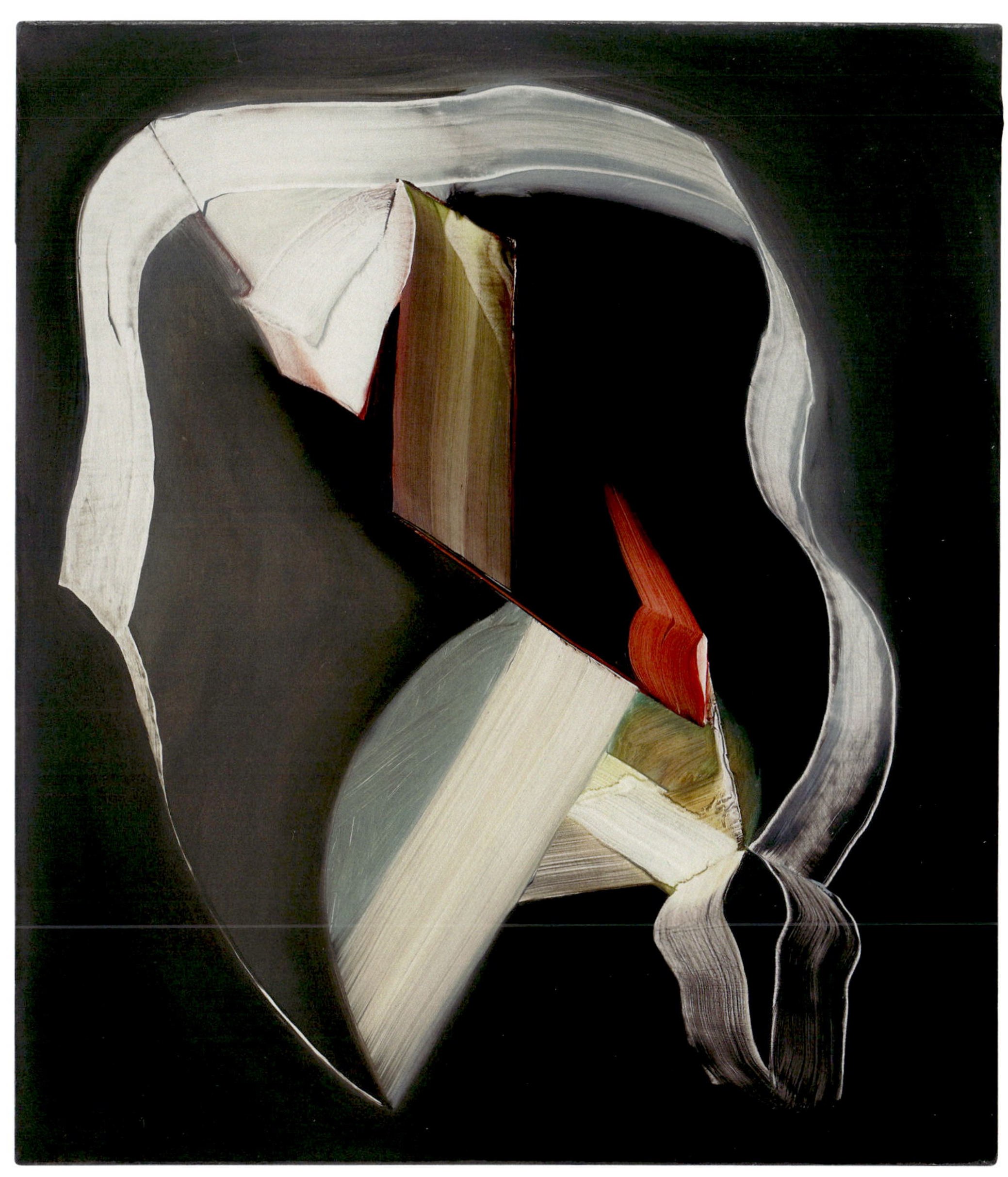

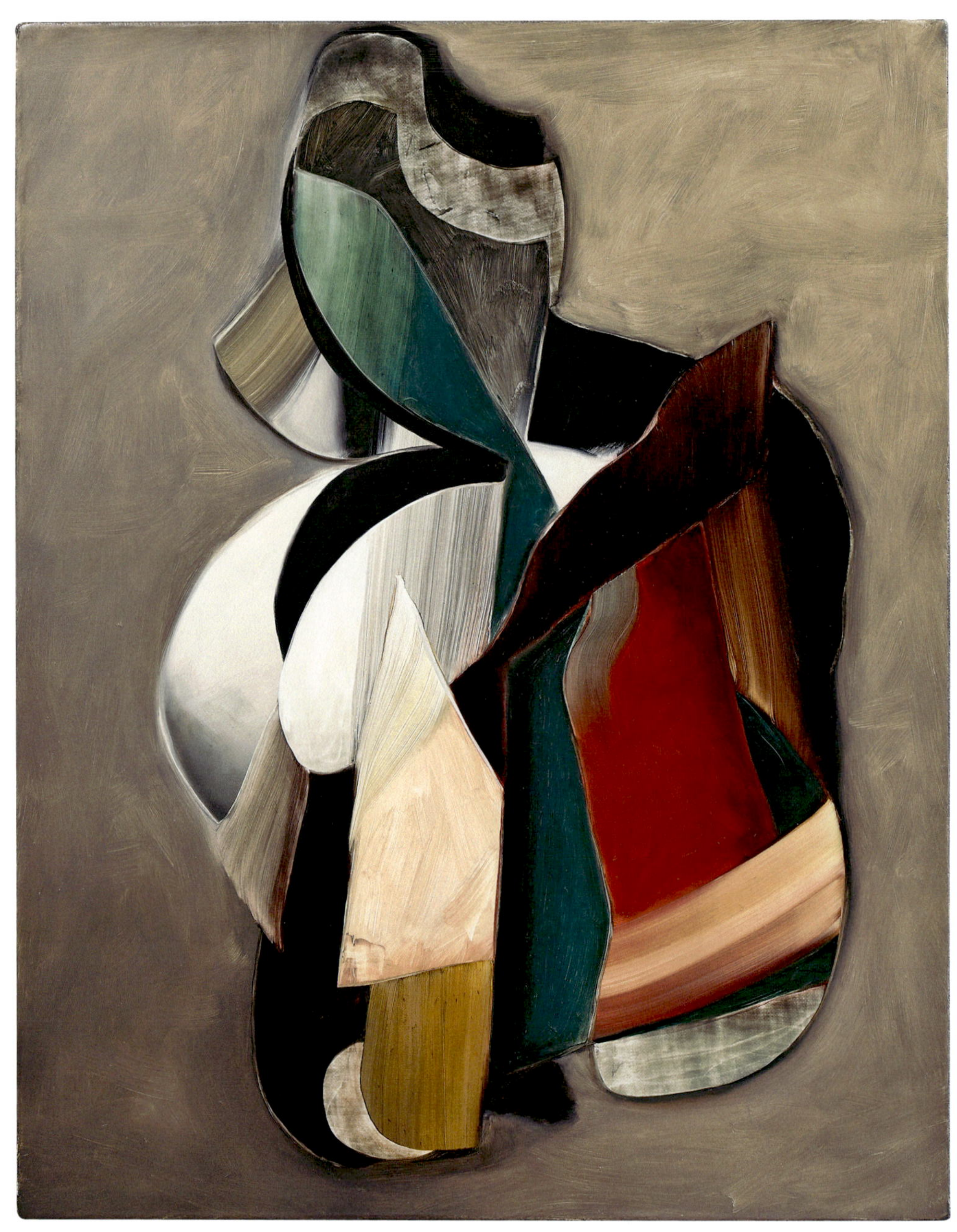

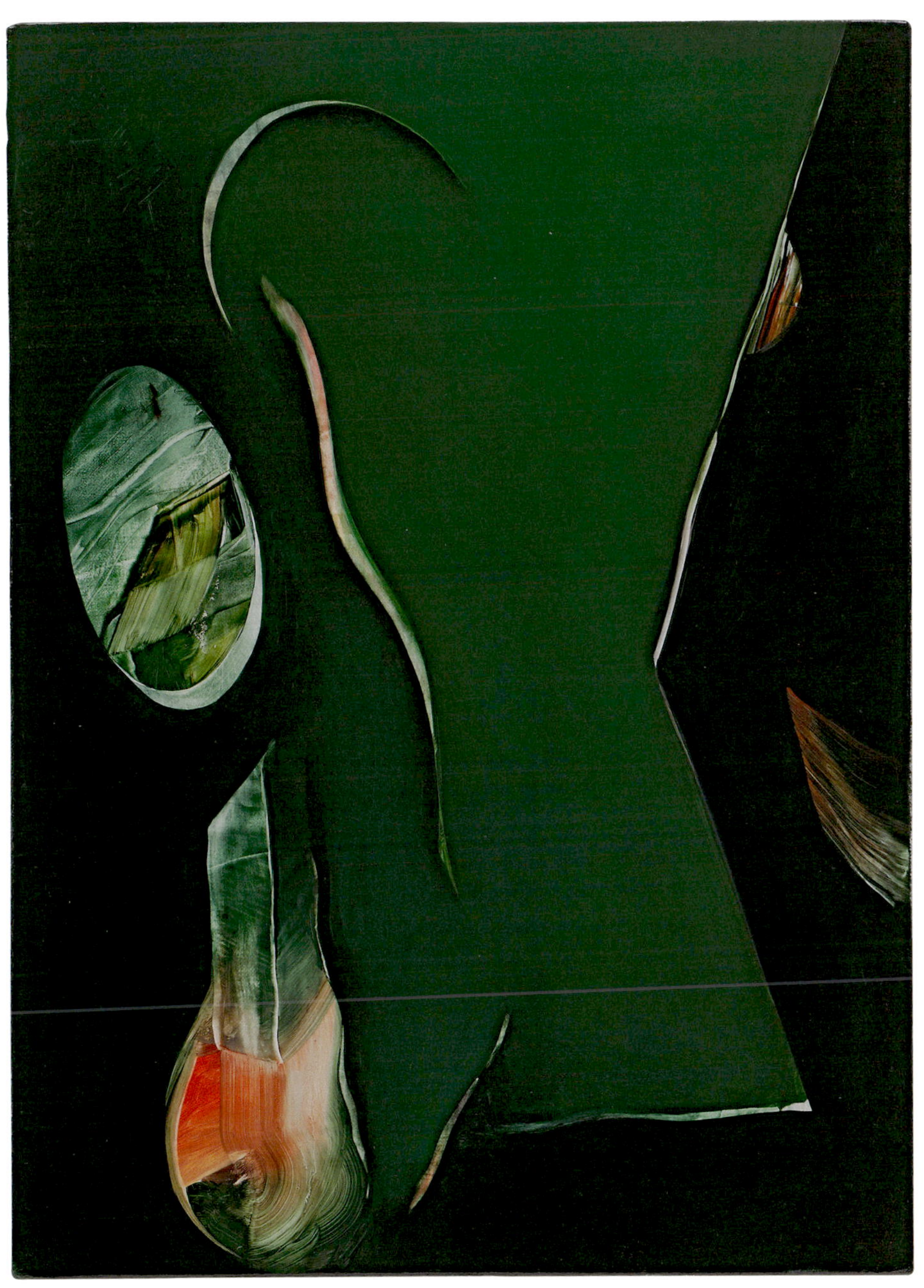

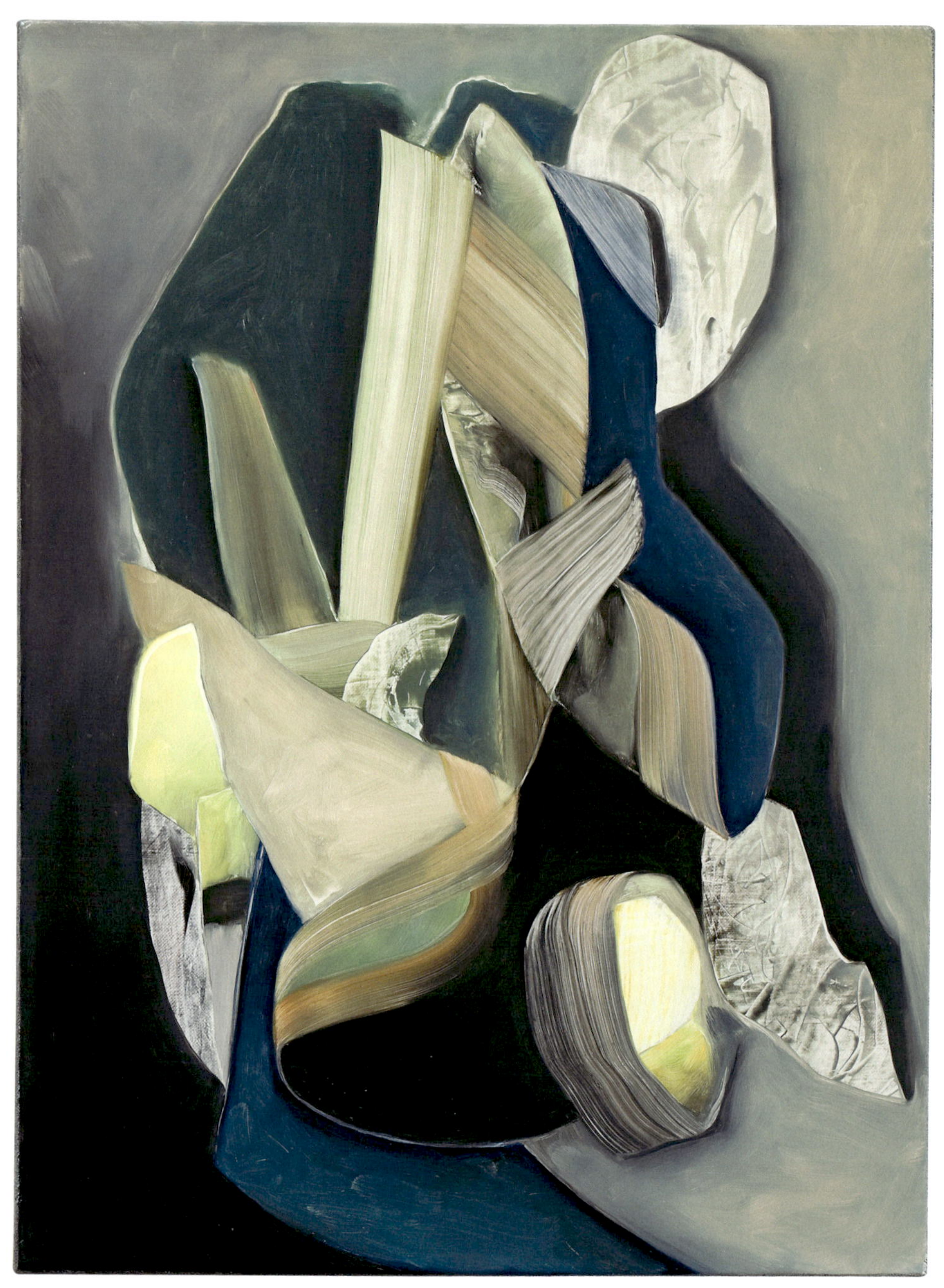

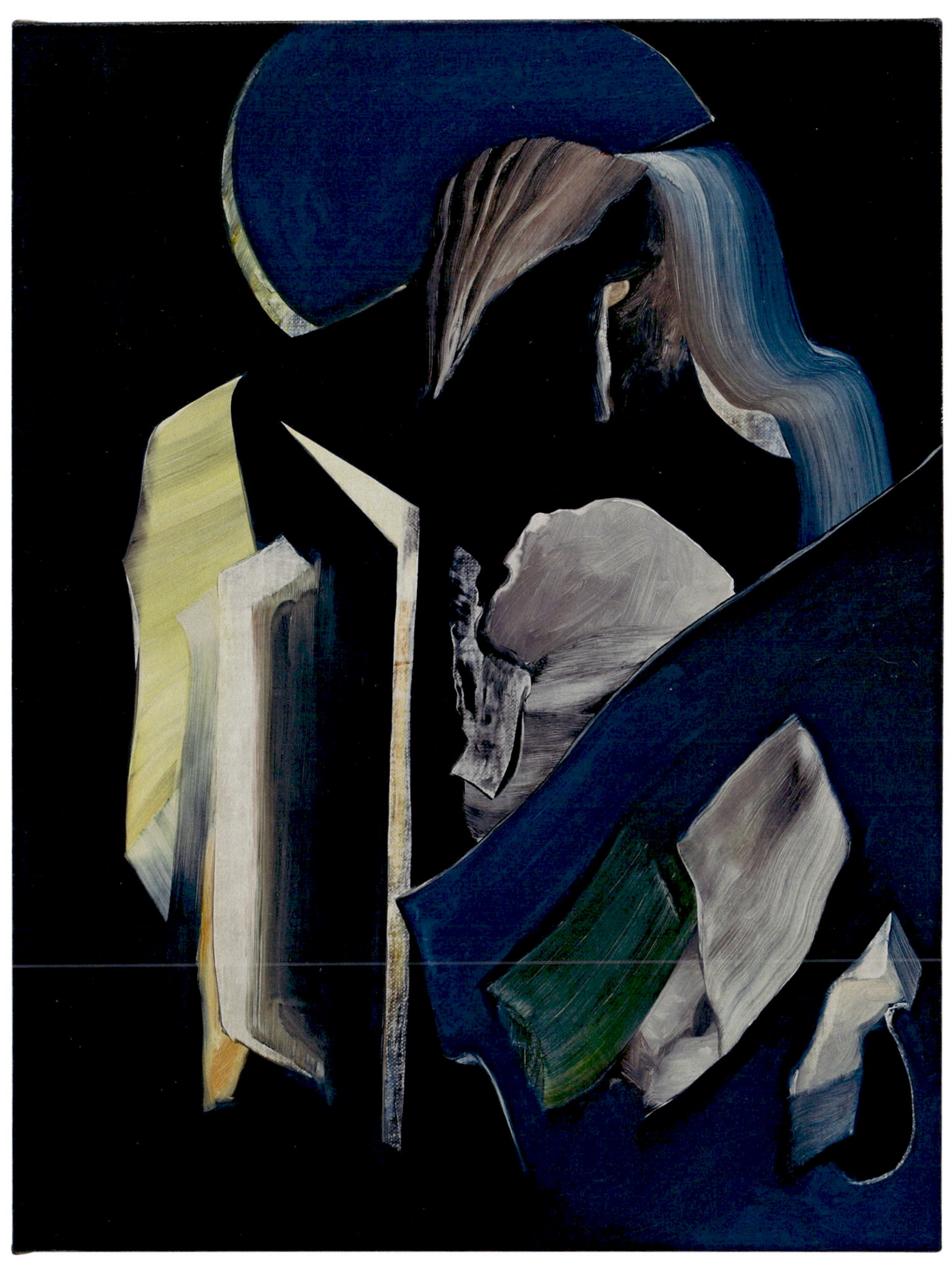

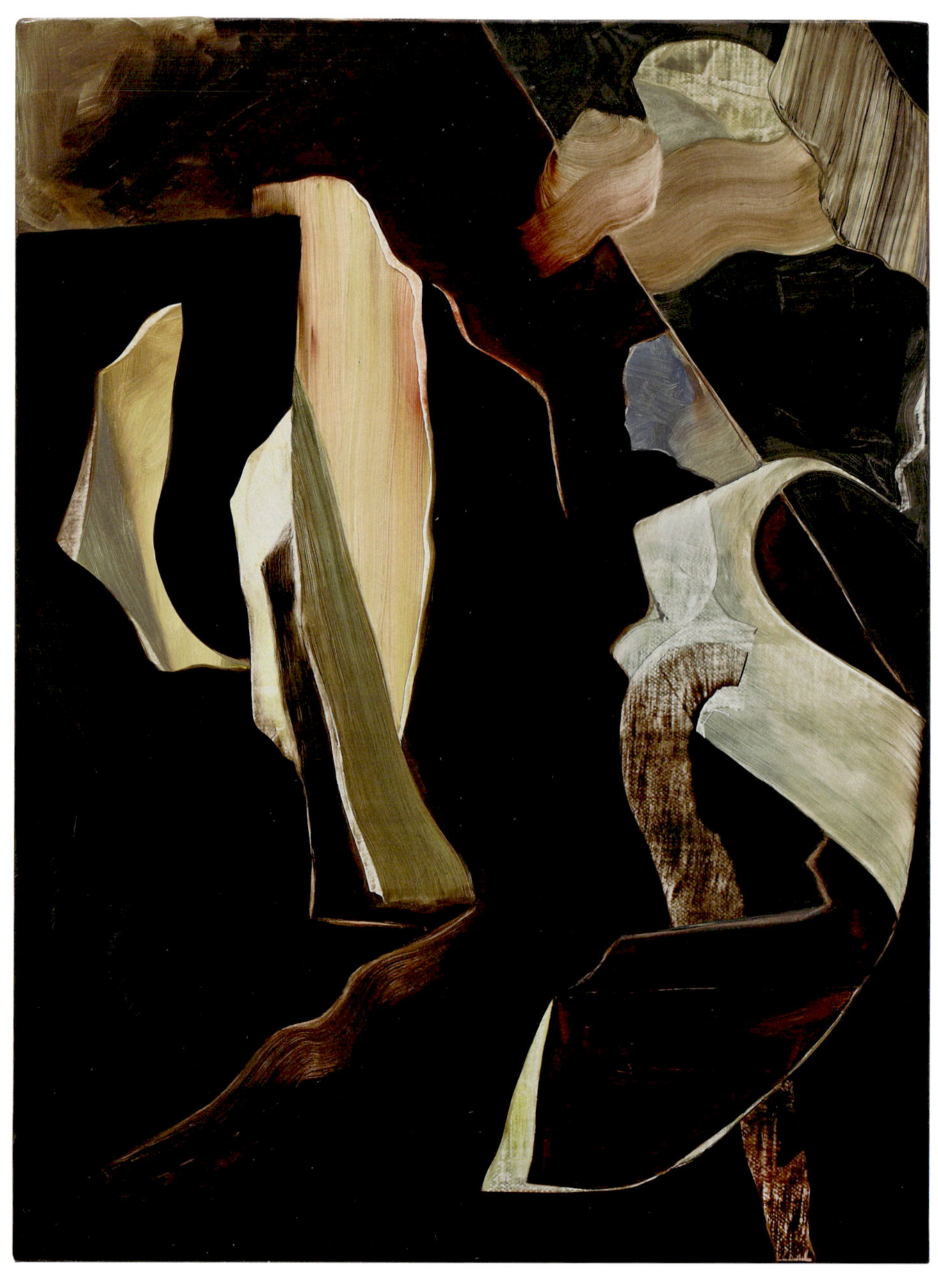

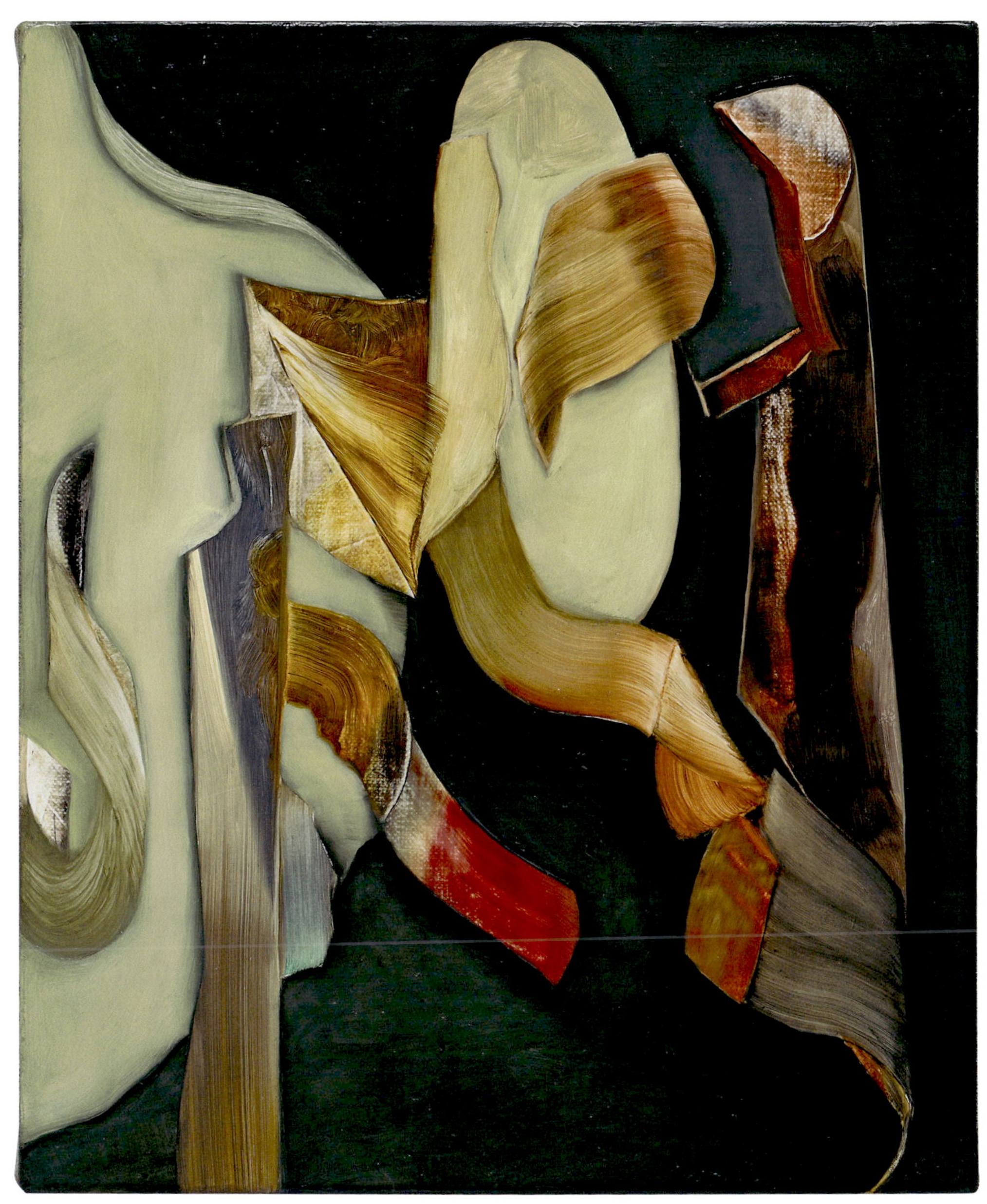

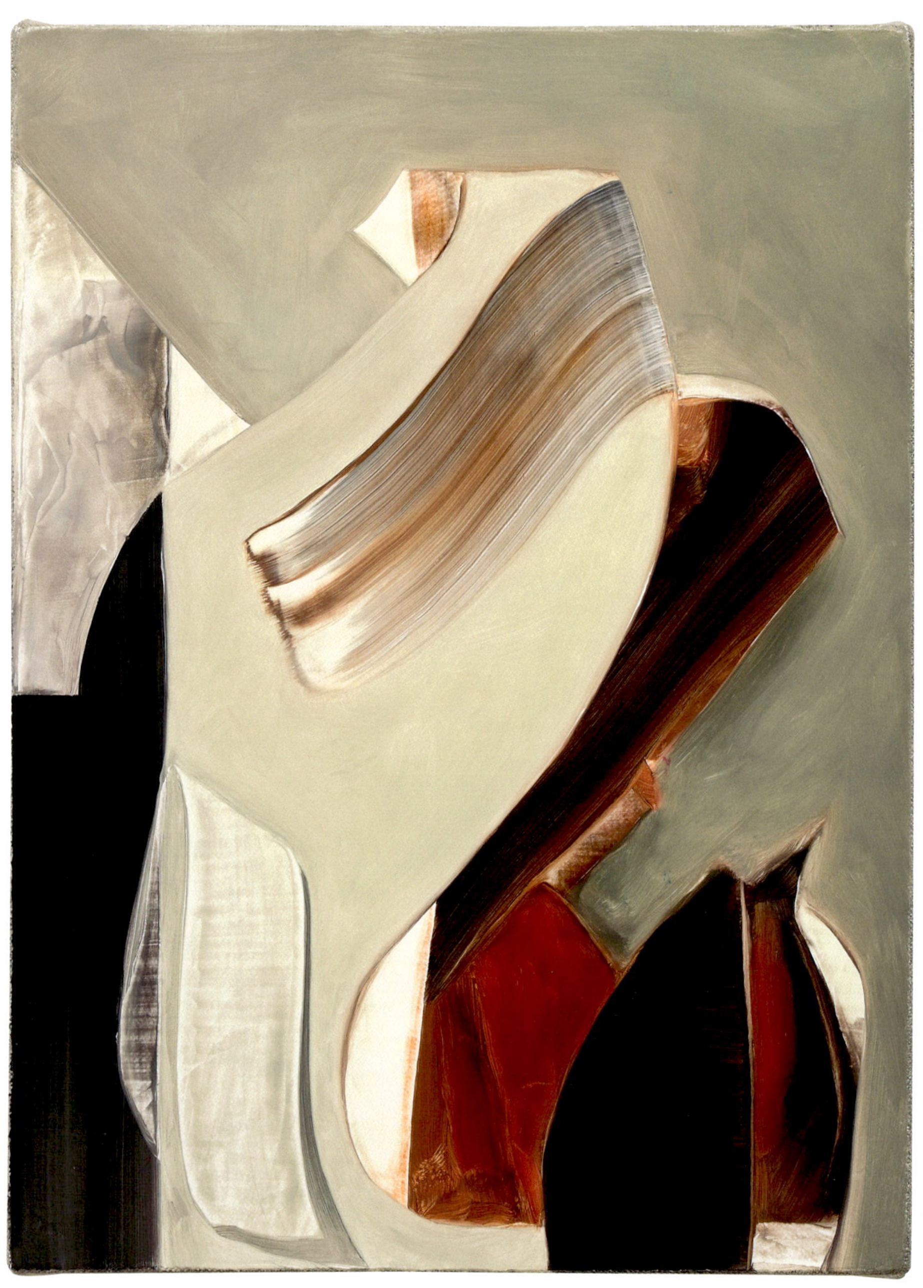

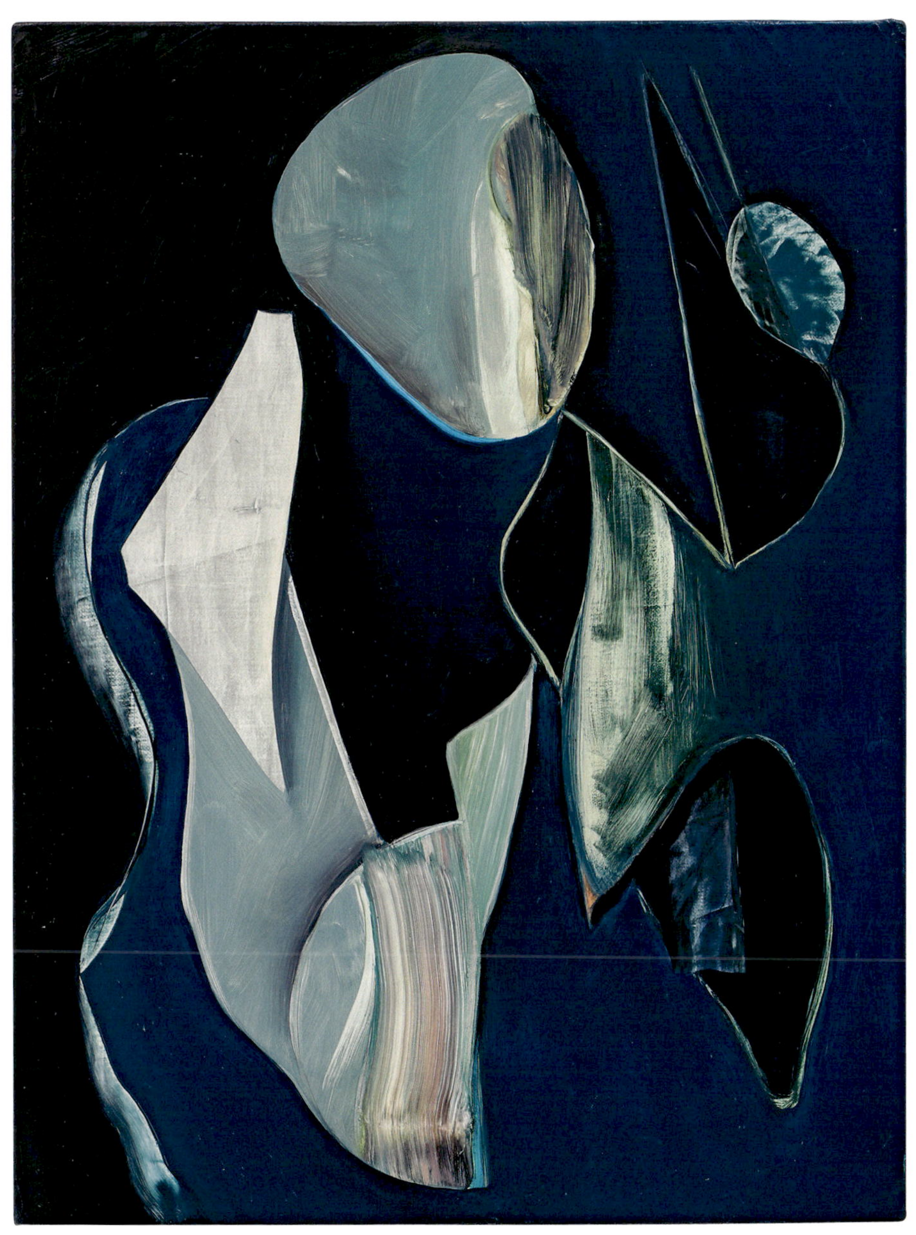

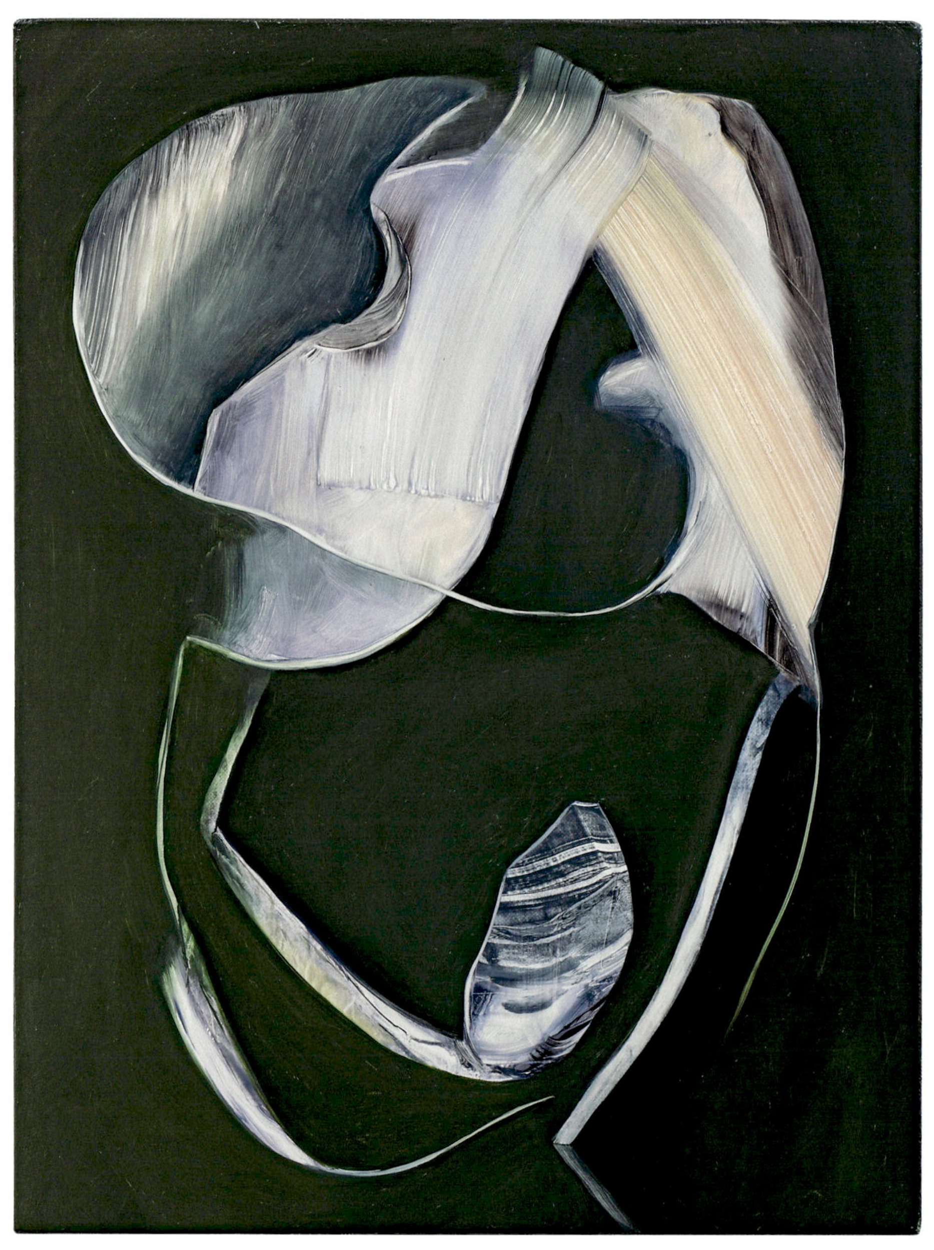

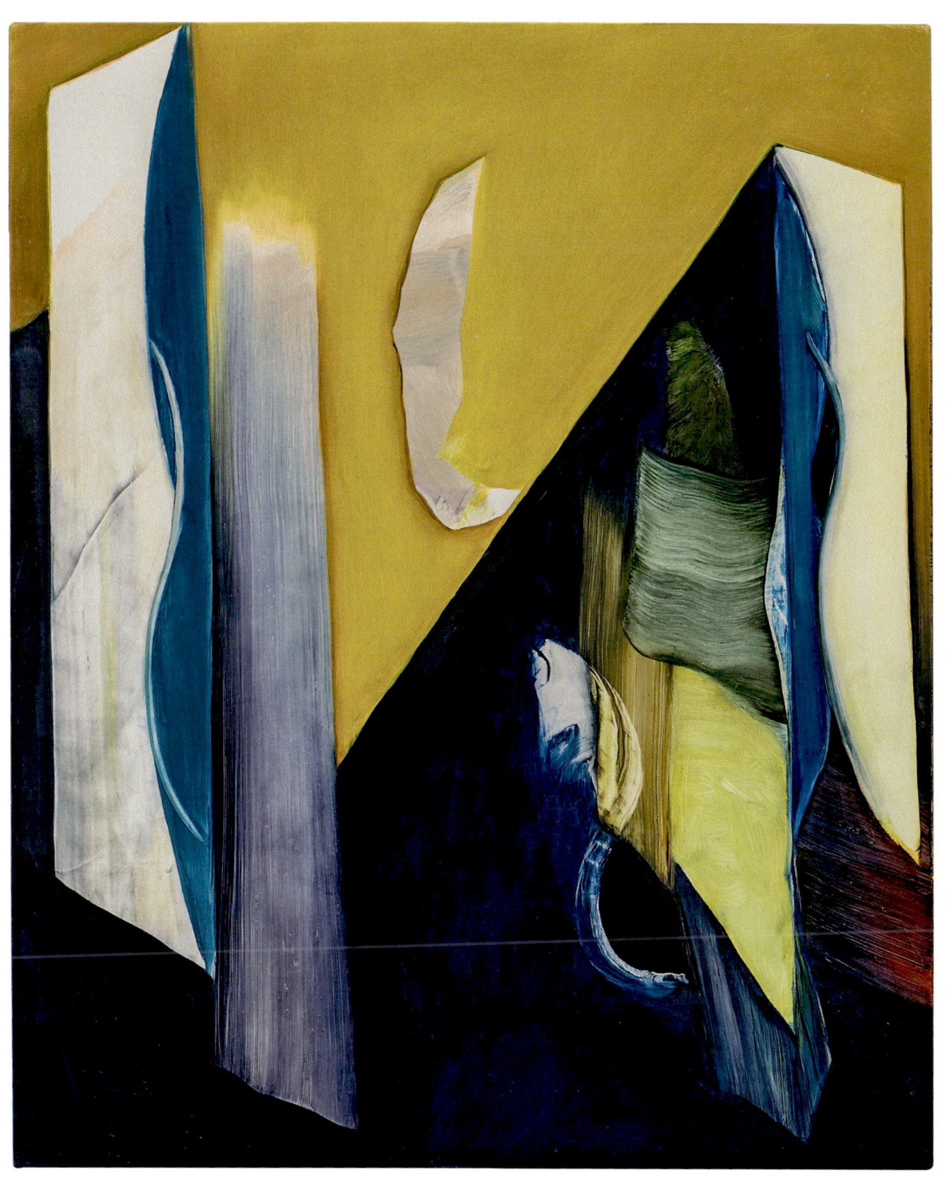

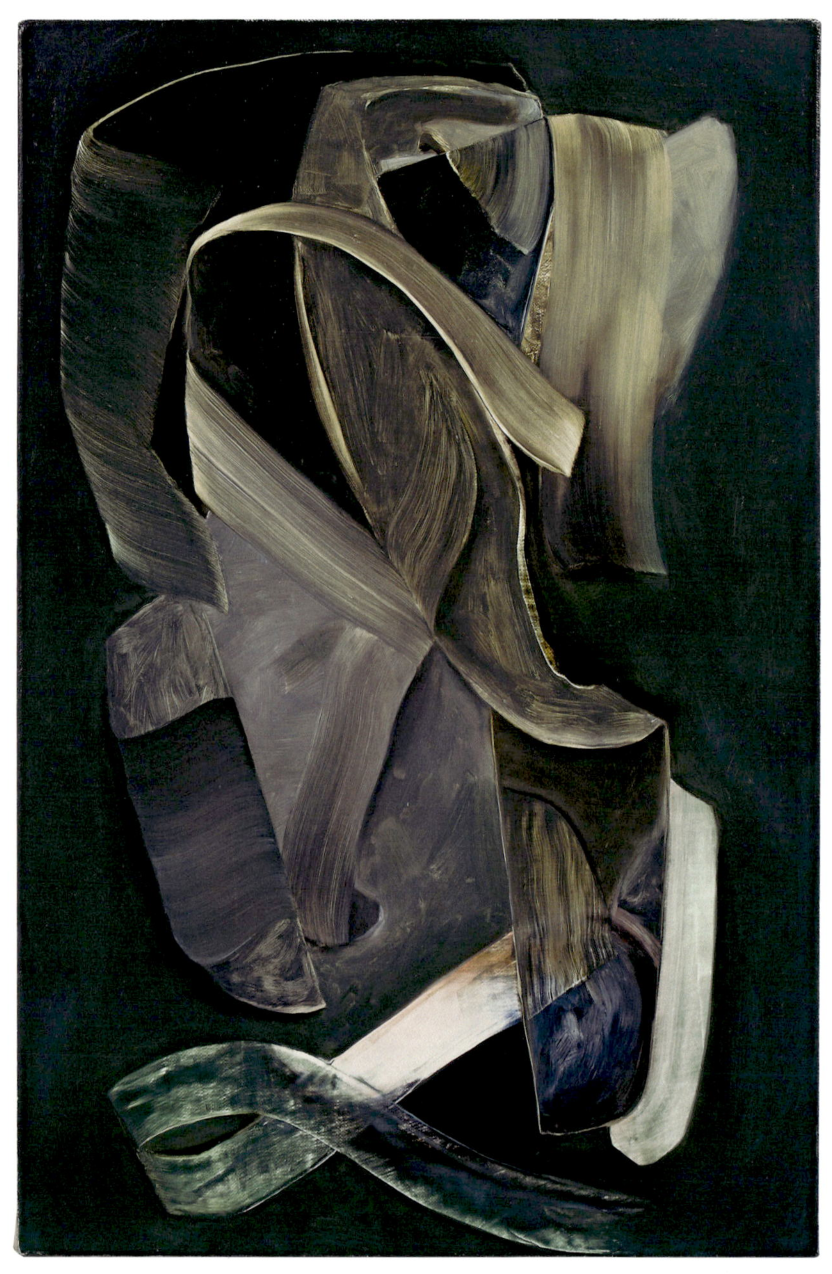

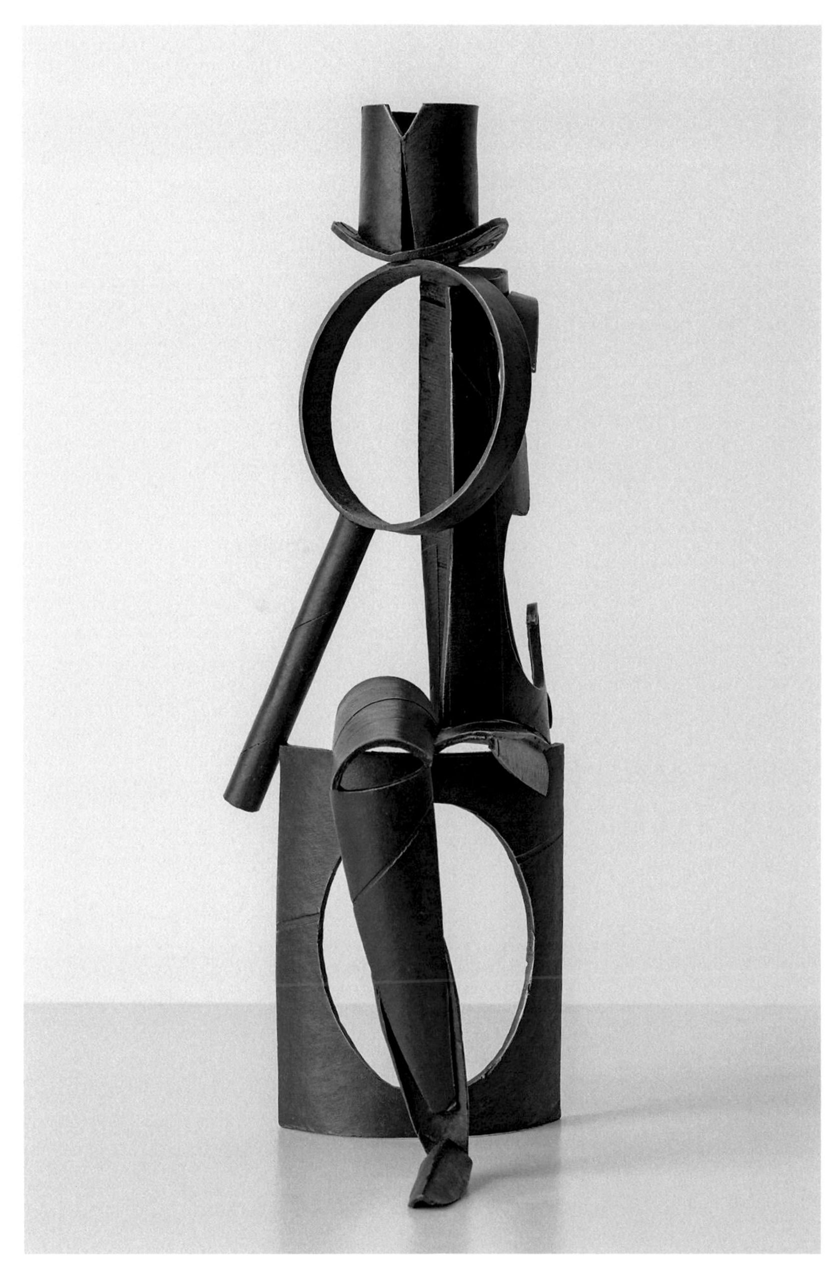

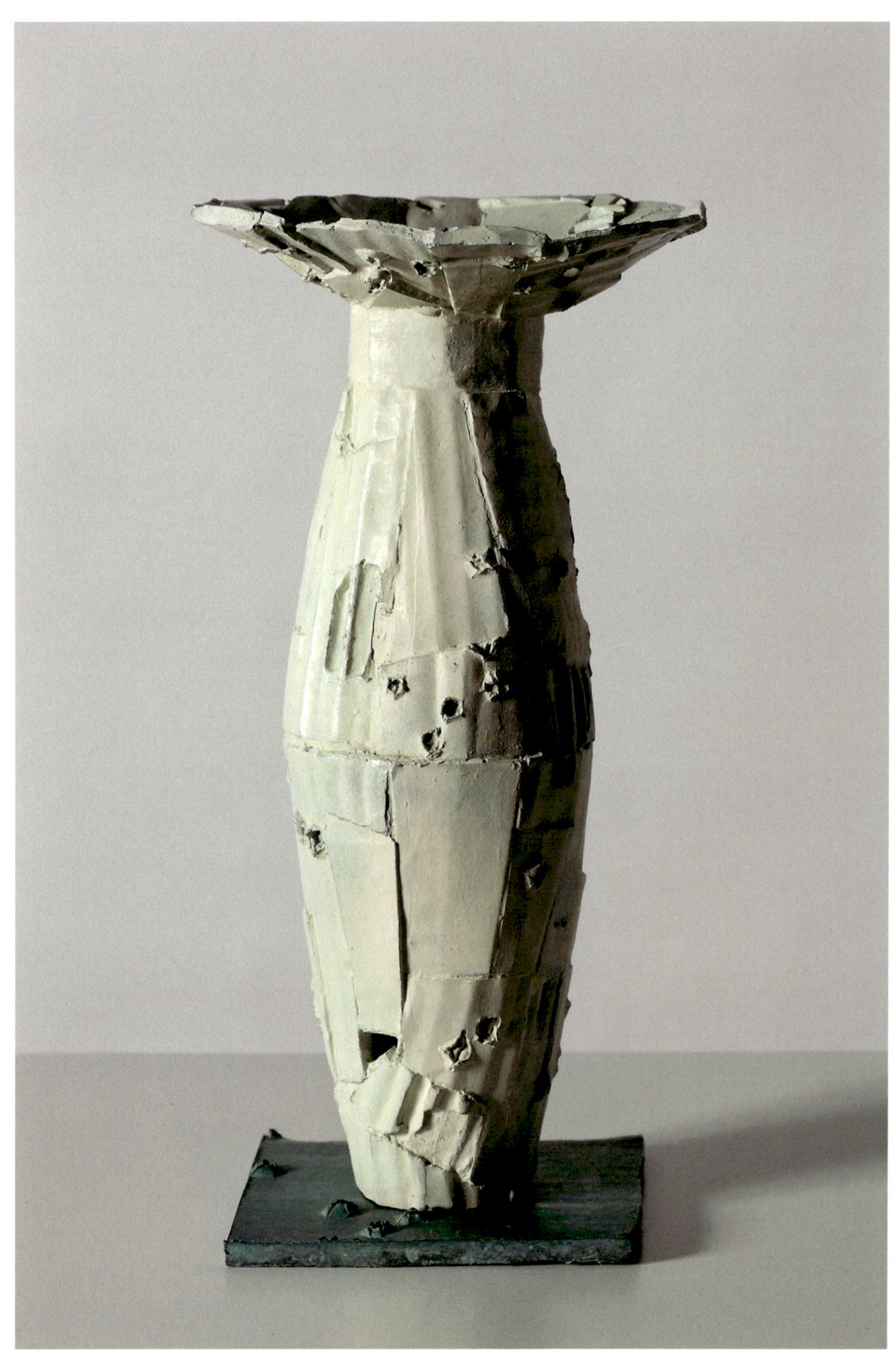

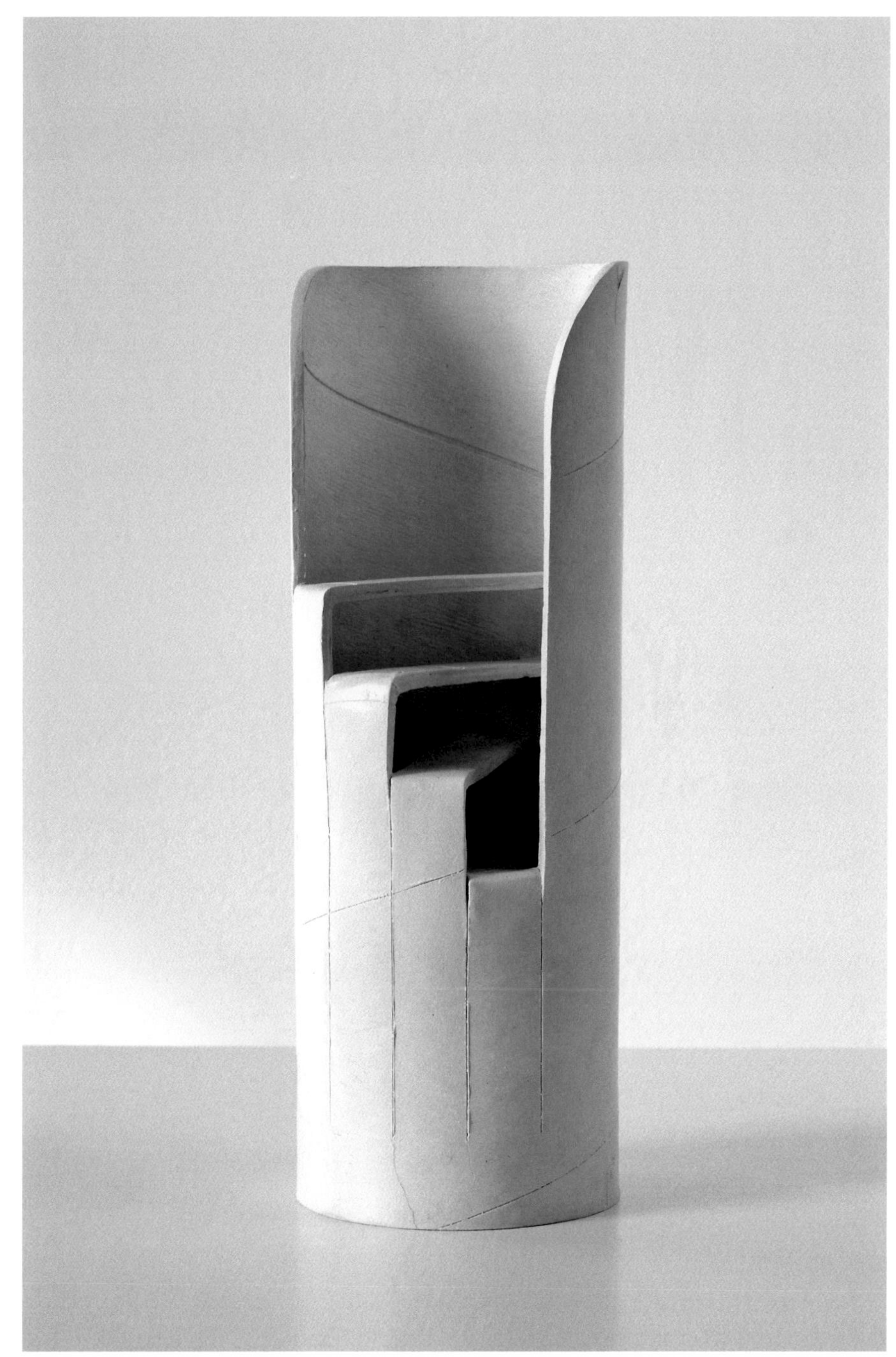

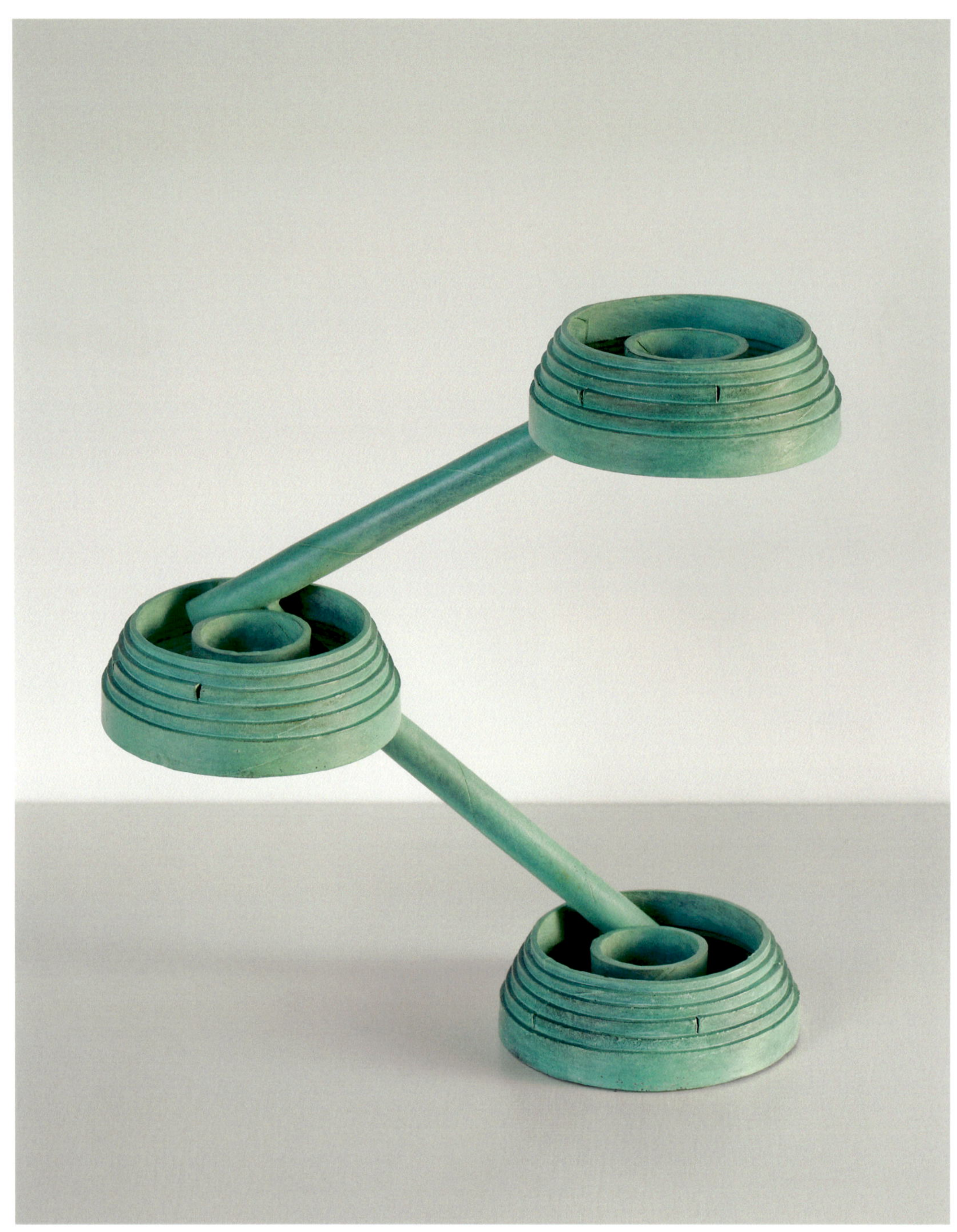

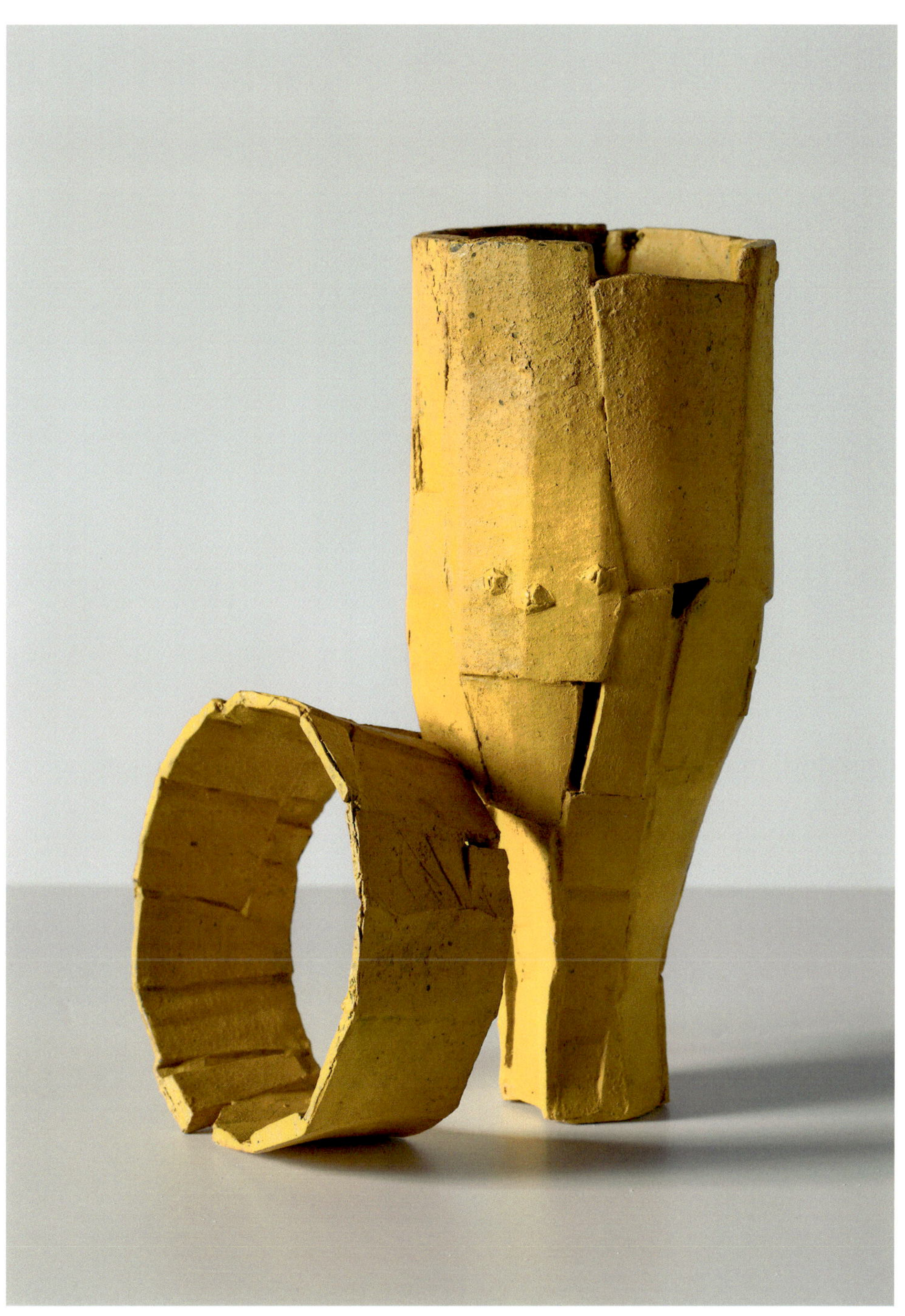

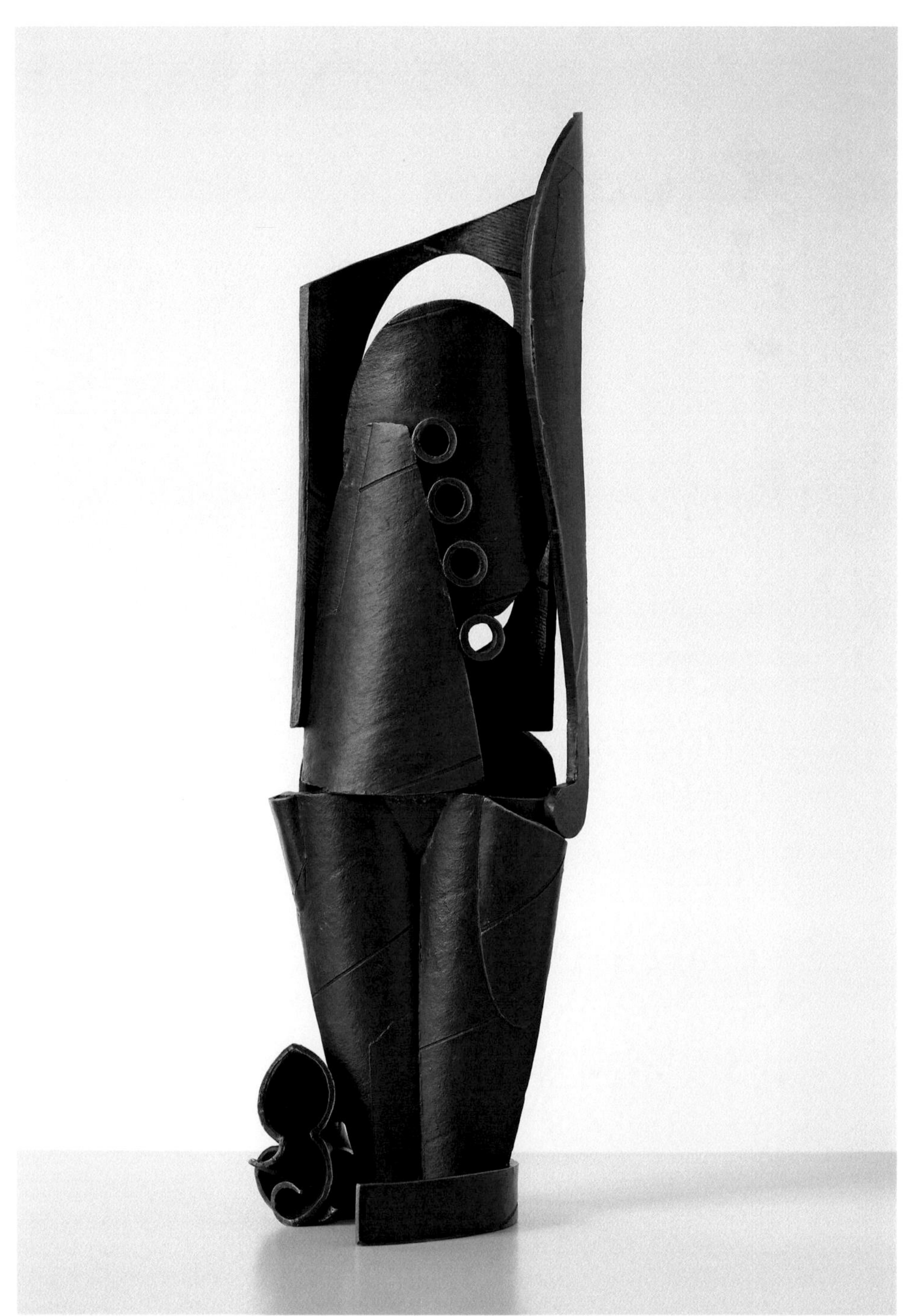

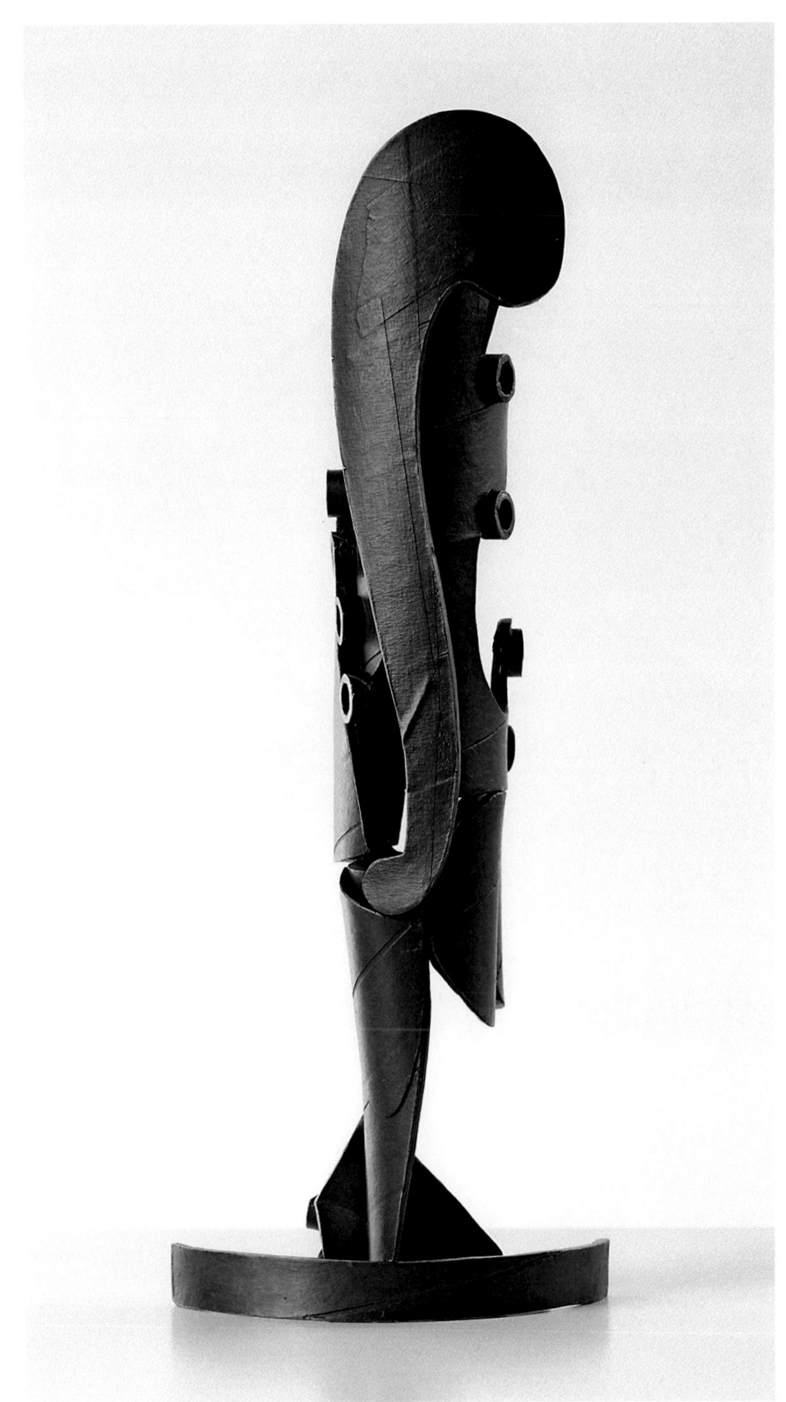

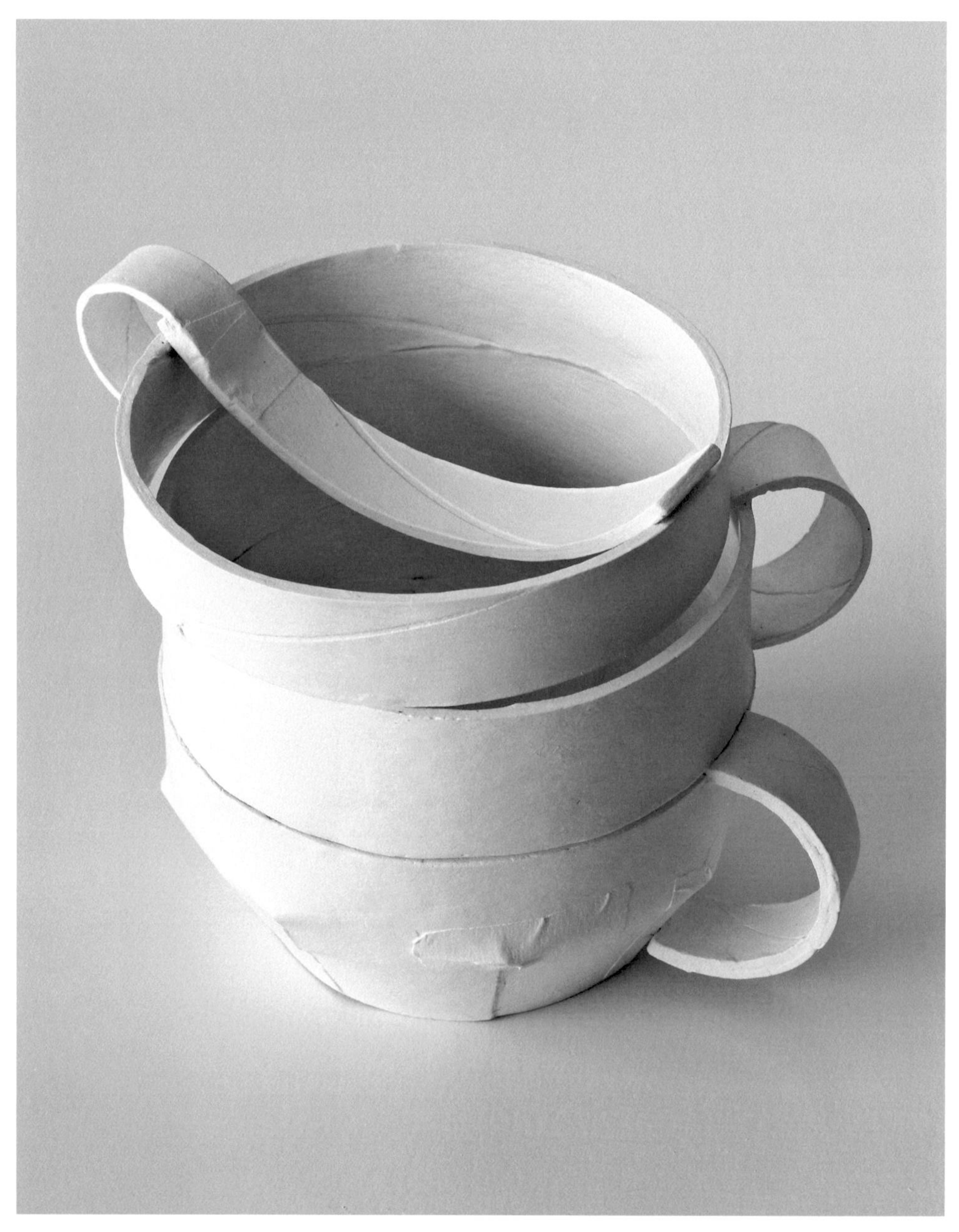

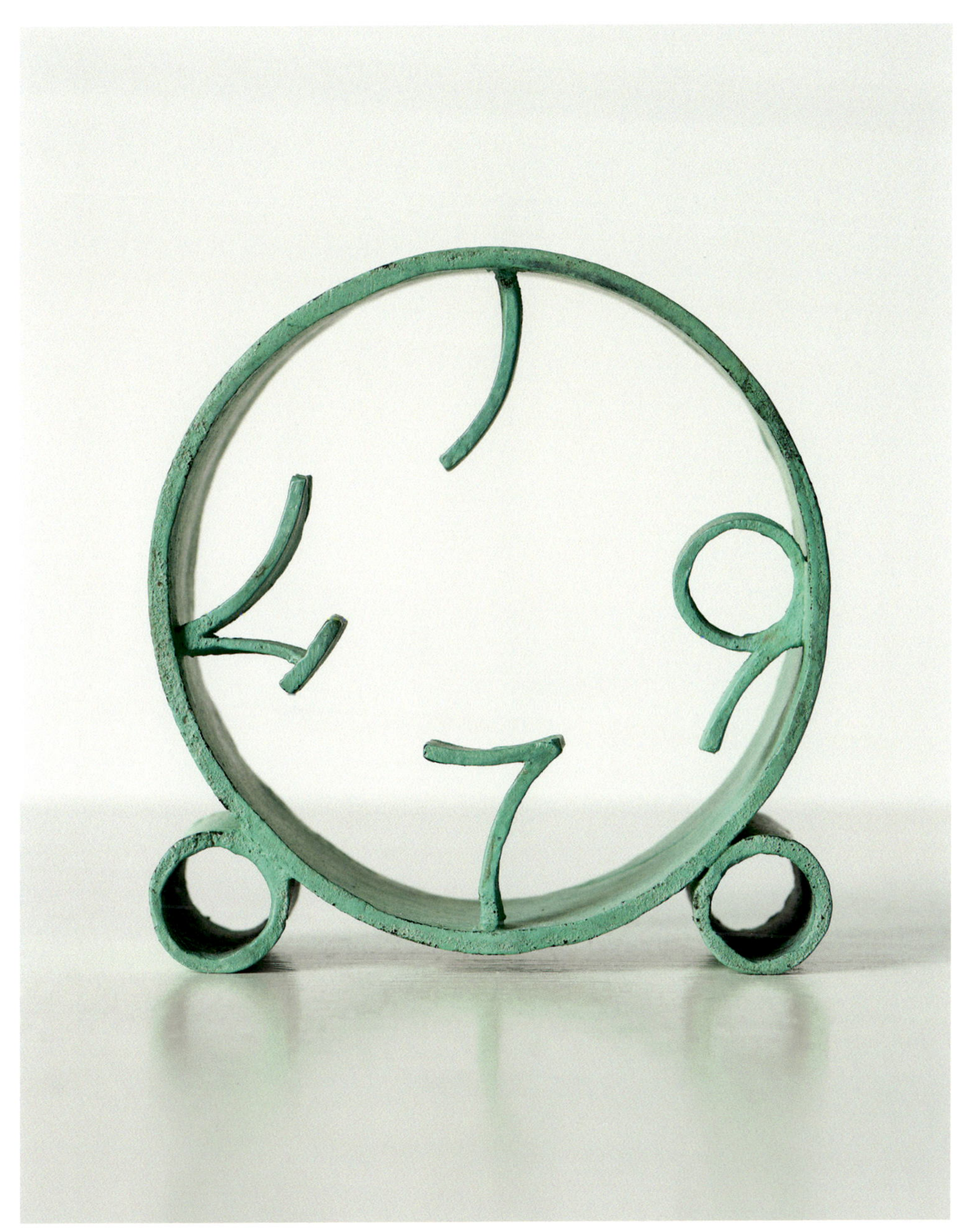

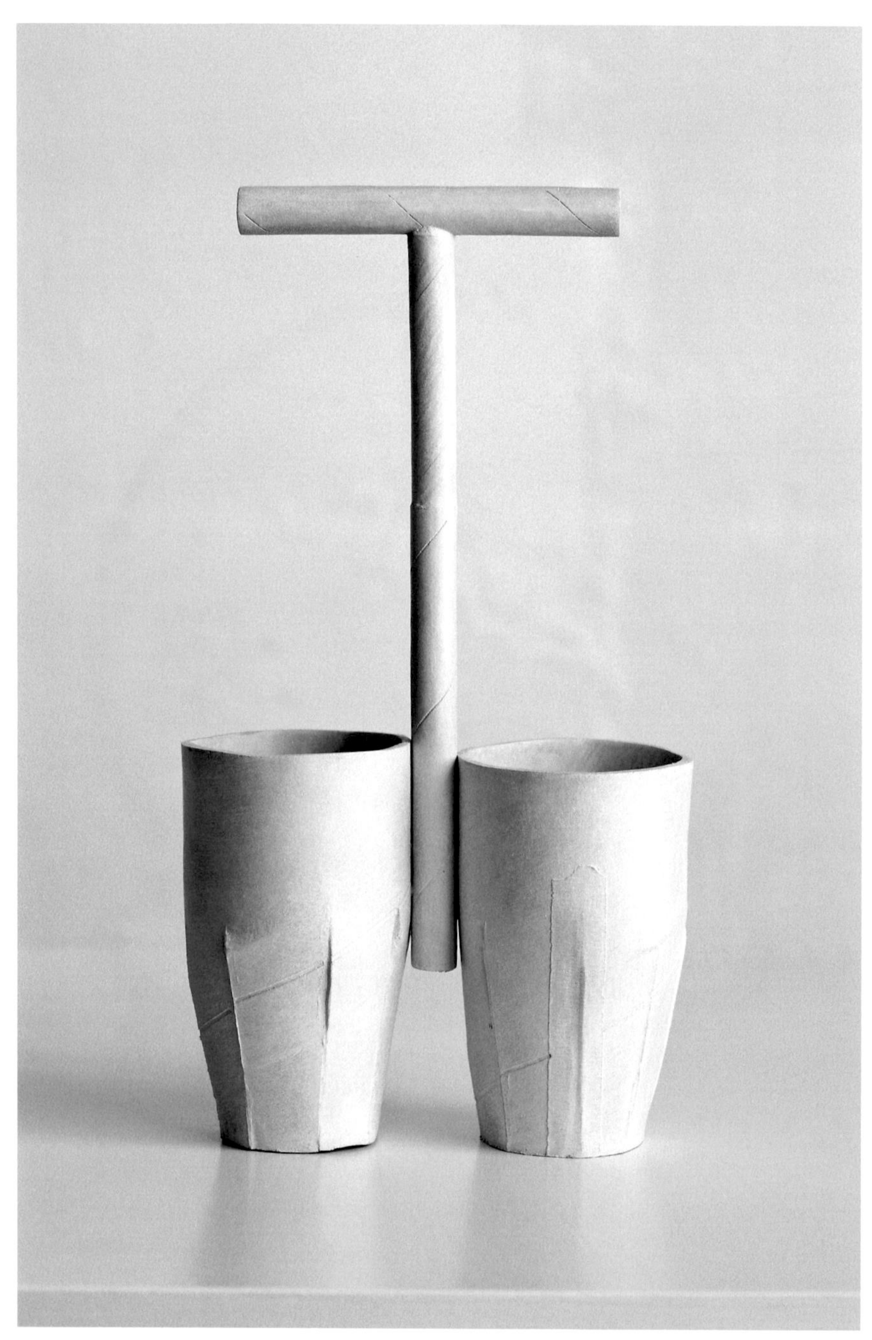

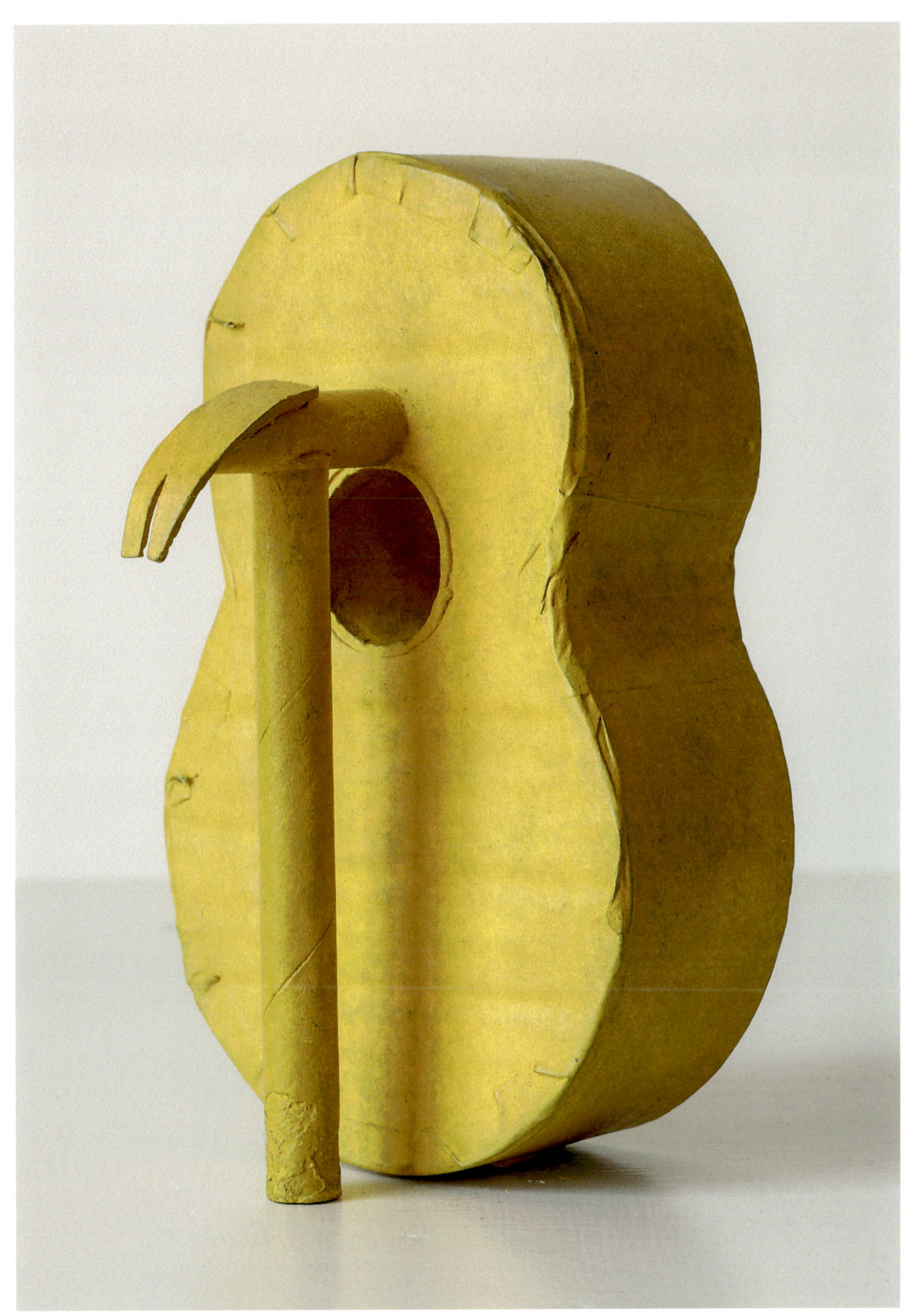

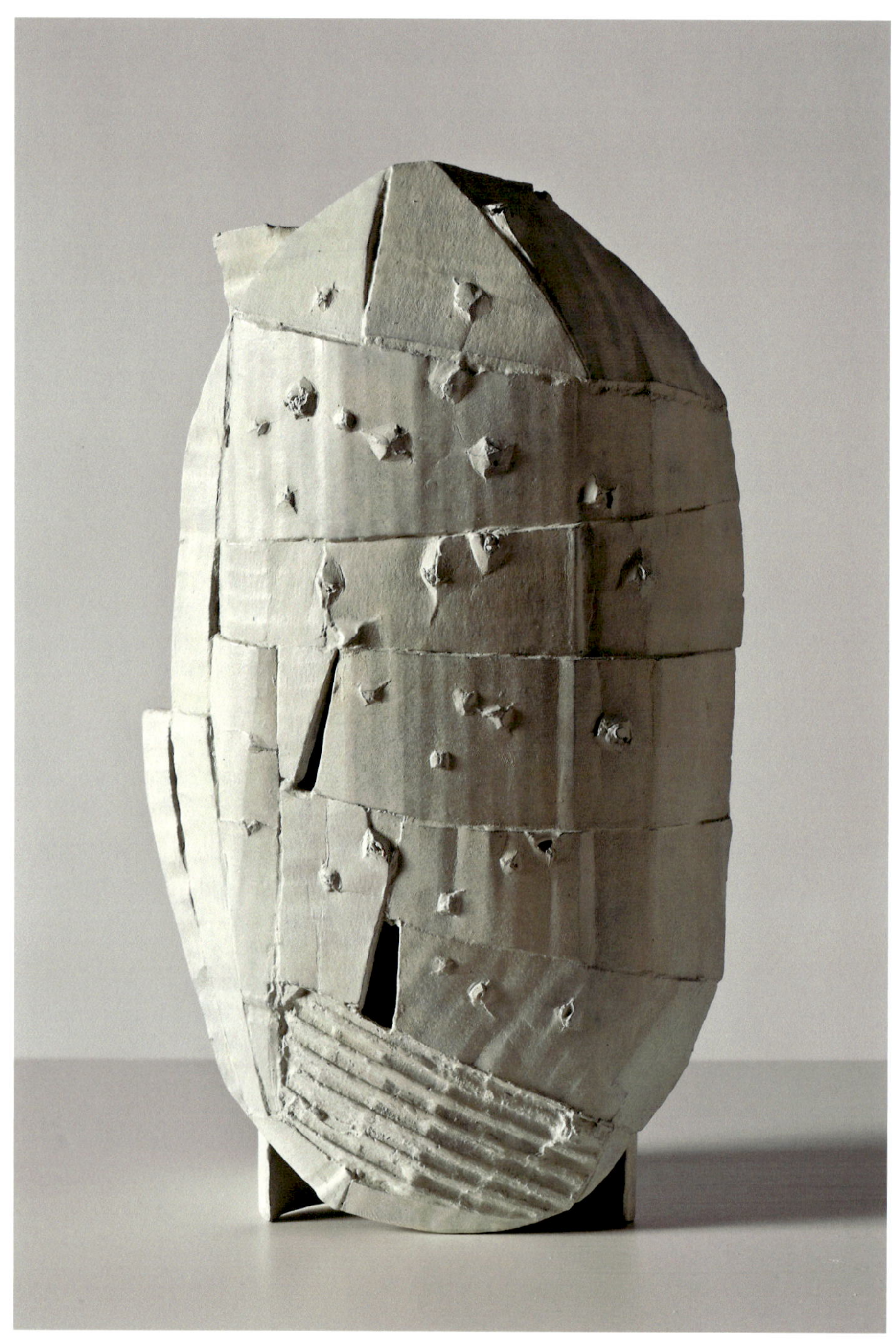

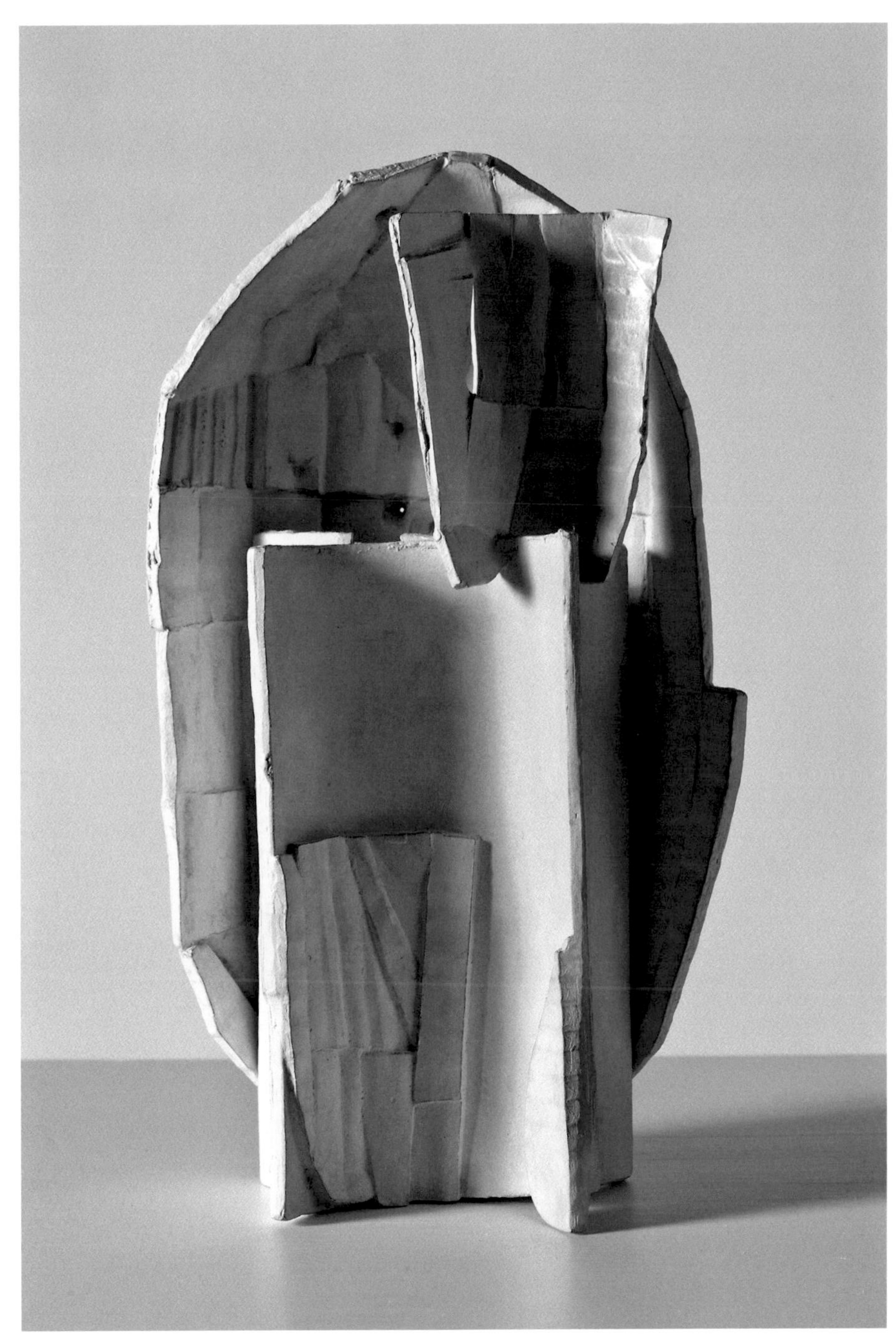

Page 28
Untitled (26)
2009
oil on linen
17 × 14 inches
Collection of Larry Sanitsky,
Beverly Hills

Page 29
Untitled (36)
2010
oil on linen
16 × 12 inches
Private Collection, Malibu

Page 30
Untitled
2011
oil on linen
14 × 10¾ inches
Collection of the artist

Page 31
Untitled (18)
2009
oil on linen
18 × 16 inches
Private Collection

Page 32
Untitled (30)
2010
oil on linen
20 × 16 inches
Private Collection

Page 33
Untitled
2012
oil on linen
19 × 14 inches

Page 34
Untitled (38)
2010
oil on linen
20 × 15 inches
Collection of John Morace and
Tom Kennedy, Los Angeles

Page 35
Untitled
2011
oil on linen
18 × 14 inches
Collection of Amanda and
Glenn Fuhrman, New York

Page 36
Untitled
2011
oil on linen
16½ × 12½ inches
UBS Art Collection

Page 37
Untitled
2011
oil on linen
12 × 10 inches
Collection of Gary Garrels and
Richard Hoblock, San Francisco

Page 38
Untitled (after Gelbe Form)
2010
oil on linen
12 × 9 inches
Rennie Collection, Vancouver

Page 39
Untitled
2012
oil on linen
19 × 14½ inches

Page 40
Untitled
2012
oil on linen
17 × 13 inches

Page 41
Untitled
2012
oil on linen
17 × 14 inches
Collection of Amanda and
Glenn Fuhrman, New York

Page 42
Untitled (48)
2010
oil on linen
21 × 14 inches
The Mario Testino Collection

Page 43
Vendor (seated)
2012
patinated bronze
15¾ × 5¾ × 9 inches
Edition of 3 + 1 AP

Page 44
Bottle/after L.R. (Bone)
2010
patinated bronze
10⅝ × 5½ × 5⅜ inches
Edition of 3 + 1 AP

Page 45
Stair Principle
2011
patinated bronze
11¾ × 4¼ × 4¼ inches
Edition of 3 + 1 AP

Page 46
Staggered Lamp Study
2011
patinated bronze
11 × 9 × 4 inches
Edition of 3 + 1 AP

Page 47
Standing Bottle with Lens (Ochre)
2011
patinated bronze
8 × 8 × 4 inches
Edition of 3 + 1 AP

Page 48
Standing Figure w/ Pockets &
Buttons
2011
patinated bronze
15½ × 4½ × 6 inches
Edition of 3 + 1 AP

Page 49
Standing Figure w/ Pockets &
Buttons (alternate view)
2011
patinated bronze
15½ × 4½ × 6 inches
Edition of 3 + 1 AP

Page 50
Magnifying Glass with Pipe
2011
patinated bronze
9 × 7 × 3⅛ inches
Edition of 3 + 1 AP

Page 51
Penguin Pots (Soot)
2011
patinated bronze
8½ × 11¾ × 2¾ inches
Edition of 3 + 1 AP

Page 52
Three-Ringed Cup (Bone)
2011
patinated bronze
5 × 6½ × 6 inches
Edition of 3 + 1 AP

Page 53
Alarm Clock Study
2011
patinated bronze
3¼ × 3¼ × 1½ inches
Edition of 3 + 1 AP

Page 54
Cups/Caddy
2011
patinated bronze
12 × 6¾ × 3 inches
Edition of 3 + 1 AP

Page 55
Retired Instruments (Yellow)
2012
patinated bronze
8½ × 4¾ × 5 inches
Unique

Page 56
Mask with Stand (Bone)
2010
patinated bronze
11½ × 6½ × 4 inches
Edition of 3 + 1 AP

Page 57
Mask with Stand (Bone)
(alternative view)
2010
patinated bronze
11½ × 6½ × 4 inches
Edition of 3 + 1 AP

Acknowledgments

Like the exhibition, this volume represents a fruitful collaboration, in this case among the artists, the co-curators, and those who produced the catalogue.

Catherine Hess is grateful to the following individuals at The Huntington for their support: Steven Koblik, President, Cristina Lutz, Associate Director for Major Gifts; Susan Turner-Lowe, Vice President for Communications; Jacqueline Dugas, Loan Registrar; Gregg Bayne, Exhibits Manager; and Susan Green and Jean Patterson, Huntington Library Press. Laurence Frank provided and continues to provide critical support in all things.

Christopher Bedford would like to thank Sherri Geldin, Director, Wexner Center for the Arts; Ann Bremner, Publications Editor, Wexner Center for the Arts; and, as ever, Jennifer Bedford for her interest, insight, and forbearance. He would like to dedicate his work on this project to his daughter, Harriet Pamela Bedford, and her grandmother and namesake, Pamela May Wulffson, who loved the Huntington.

Catherine and Christopher also thank Lesley Vance and Ricky Swallow for their vision and dedication and, for their support, Laura and Carlton Seaver, Nancy Berman, Margery and Maurice Katz, David Kordansky Gallery, Los Angeles; Stuart Shave/Modern Art, London; and Marc Foxx Gallery and Rodney Hill, Los Angeles. At Marquand Books, Adrian Lucia, Jeff Wincapaw, Ryan Polich, Brynn Warriner, and Leah Finger constituted a talented and supportive team. Thanks are also due to designer Zach Hooker and editor Martin Fox. Catherine is indebted to Christopher and he to her: without the insight, energy, and perseverance of both, this project would have languished.

Ricky Swallow and Lesley Vance wish to thank the following people for their support: Chris Bedford, Catherine Hess, Suzanne Hudson, Stuart Shave, David Kordansky, Marc Foxx, Jimi Lee, Rodney Hill, Mike Homer, Alexis Kerin, Fredrik Nilsen, Ian Killips and the team at Art Bronze Inc. Burbank, Blackwidow LLC, Los Angeles, Cranston Montgomery, Michael Ned Holte, Andy Beach, Ryan Conder, Lenny, and, as always, each other.